BOOKS BY THOMAS C. ODEN

AFTER MODERNITY . . . WHAT?
AFTER THERAPY WHAT?
AGENDA FOR THEOLOGY
BECOMING A MINISTER
BEYOND REVOLUTION
CARE OF SOULS IN THE CLASSIC TRADITION
THE COMMUNITY OF CELEBRATION
CONSCIENCE AND DIVIDENDS
CONTEMPORARY THEOLOGY AND PSYCHOTHERAPY
CRISIS MINISTRIES
DOCTRINAL STANDARDS IN THE WESLEYAN TRADITION
GAME FREE
GUILT FREE
THE INTENSIVE GROUP EXPERIENCE: THE NEW PIETISM
KERYGMA AND COUNSELING
MINISTRY THROUGH WORD AND SACRAMENT
THE PARABLES OF KIERKEGAARD
PASTORAL THEOLOGY
PHOEBE PALMER: SELECTED WRITINGS
THE PROMISE OF BARTH: THE ETHICS OF FREEDOM
RADICAL OBEDIENCE: THE ETHICS OF RUDOLF BULTMANN
SHOULD TREATMENT BE TERMINATED?
THE STRUCTURE OF AWARENESS
SYSTEMATIC THEOLOGY

TWO WORLDS

NOTES ON THE DEATH OF MODERNITY
IN AMERICA & RUSSIA

Thomas C. Oden

INTERVARSITY PRESS
DOWNERS GROVE, ILLINOIS 60515

InterVarsity Press is the book-publishing division of Inter-Varsity Christian Fellowship, a student movement active on campus at hundreds of universities, colleges and schools of nursing in the United States of America, and a member movement of the International Fellowship of Evangelical Students. For information about local and regional activities, write Public Relations Dept., InterVarsity Christian Fellowship, 6400 Schroeder Rd., P.O. Box 7895, Madison, WI 53707-7895.

All Scripture quotations, unless otherwise indicated, are from the HOLY BIBLE, NEW INTERNATIONAL VERSION. Copyright © 1973, 1978, 1984 International Bible Society. Used by permission of Zondervan Publishing House. All rights reserved.

Cover illustration: Roberta Polfus

ISBN 0-8308-1763-8

Printed in the United States of America

Library of Congress Cataloging-in-Publication Data

Oden, Thomas C.
   Two worlds: notes on the death of modernity in America and
Russia / Thomas C. Oden.
      p.   cm.
   Includes bibliographical references.
   ISBN 0-8308-1763-8
   1. Postmodernism—Religious aspects—Christianity.
2. Theology—20th century. 3. United States—Church history—20th
century. 4. Soviet Union—Church history—1917- 5. Oden, Thomas
C.—Journeys—Soviet Union. 6. Soviet Union—Description and
travel—1970- 7. Religion—Study and teaching—Soviet Union—
History—20th century. I. Title.
BT28.O34   1992
274.7'0829—dc20

91-37117
CIP

17 16 15 14 13 12 11 10 9 8 7 6 5 4 3 2 1
06 05 04 03 02 01 00 99 98 97 96 95 94 93 92

For Laura

Preface: First World, Second World

The notion of the "Third World" assumes a first and second world. It is on the spiritual ordeal of these two worlds that our attention focuses. The struggle of the Third World is affected signIficantly by what happens in the quality of relations between the First and Second Worlds, how accurately each discerns the other's intent. The fluctuating idea of a Second World is even more diffuse and extensive than either Russia or the former Soviet Union. It embraces all those former client states once decisively mothered by Soviet policy from Moscow.

What used to be a cohesive Soviet Union is now a disintegrating Soviet system. Since *Soviet* identifies the old order before the failed coup, wherever *Soviet* appears in what follows, I ask you to think of the lapsed predecessor Soviet society. As this manuscript was being written there still was a Soviet Union. At its time of publication, the Soviet Union is ceasing to exist as a political entity, and becoming a loose confederation of republics. Yet the naming of the new entity has not been settled. At press time we still had no new and widely accepted designation for the USSR, or Soviet Union. Such tricks of timing make it even more difficult to write about these difficult enough subjects. So during this transitional period, it seems better to ask the reader implicitly to read "former Soviet Union" where the terms *Soviet Union* or *USSR* appear, rather than repeatedly intruding the word *former* in the text (or inserting something like Union of Sovereign Eurasian States, which is still in process of being defined).

The category that best describes the current Russian situation is paradox. Whatever one can conceive of saying about it, one soon finds oneself saying virtually the opposite to seek a proximate balance.

I am indebted to Daryl McCarthy of the International Institute for Christian Studies, who first challenged me to go to the Soviet Union; to Kent Hill and Mark Elliott for excellent advice in preparation for the visits; to Igor Yablokov and Alexander Krasnikov for hosting me graciously in Moscow; to Rodney Clapp for careful and timely editing of the manuscript; and above all my daughter Laura, who figures most profoundly in my personal sense of calling to the Soviet Union. I am especially grateful that one of my closest colleagues, Dr. Daniel B. Clendenin, formerly of Drew University Graduate School, is now teaching in Christian Studies in Moscow State University.

Introduction

The unexpected invitation to lecture in the Soviet Union came from the very professors once charged with intellectually defending official Soviet atheism—the former Department of Atheism of Moscow State University. Since glasnost, its new name is the Department of Scientific and Historical Study of Religion and Freethinking.

The name change represents a fundamental reassignment of resources in the Philosophy section of the Humanities Division of this immense university. The alteration is more than cosmetic. The university study of religion in the Soviet Union is no longer a compliant agent of atheistic ideology but now is appearing to be much more like what we would call the comparative study of religion. Once the pampered proxy of official atheistic ideology, this department is now being required to make it on its own merits amid the precarious intellectual competition of the university.

What follows is a brief report in a personal voice that makes no claim whatever of being more than ephemeral anecdotal evidence. Though it offers only a small slice of personal experience, within that frame of reference I must say that I have never before found myself in a place where I felt that events were mirroring more sharply some decisive moment of historical change.

These two giant, quintessentially modern societies, Soviet and American, seemed to me to be surprisingly similar at one level, for they were both suffering from the rapidly deteriorating assumptions of modernity. While in the US modernity has taken the form of idolatrous individualism and in the USSR it has taken the form of idolatrous collectivism, it is in both cases a false understanding of autonomy that is now collapsing into whatever it is that is following the modern period (1789 to 1989, French Revolution to the collapse of Marxism). I call it postmodernity. In both societies the remnants of Enlightenment optimism, scientism, and hedonism now rot and suffer. Despite enormous differences, both Soviet and American societies are grieving over the decomposing assumptions of modern nihilistic relativism.

As late as November, 1986, even Gorbachev was still dutifully calling for an "uncompromising struggle against manifestations of religion." Within the last few years, fresh winds appear to be blowing in Soviet universities, creating a new climate for religious studies.

Now it appears that a once unbending atheistic society is looking with quiet desperation for ways to incorporate the vitality of religious understandings and communities and sacramental life into its common ethos. It no longer appears to be actively resisting religion, but rather look longingly to religion to help stabilize a highly destabilized social environment.

I had agreed to lecture to undergraduate students on the theme of postmodern Christian consciousness, and to doctoral students on the structure of awareness in time. I intended to develop and interpret for a Soviet audience some of the basic arguments found in two of my books, *After Modernity . . . What?* and *The Structure of Awareness.* Actually much more developed, as will become clear in the pages that follow.

It took some pondering for me to realize why I felt so inwardly called to take on this assignment. In time I uncovered two layers of motivations: First, I wanted to test my evangelical-patristic vocation in a non-Protestant environment. That is partly why I spent several weeks in Rome before going to Moscow. I gradually discovered that my vocation, with very little reconceptualization, was as valid and relevant in Rome or Moscow as within my native Protestant American ethos.

Second, I wanted to try to grasp the cross-cultural implication of the interpretation of the death of modernity and birth of postmodernity that I had worked out largely within the context of Protestantism. I felt that the Soviet Union was a spectacularly diverse cultural environment in which to examine whether what I had been saying about postmodernity might be more broadly applicable within a very different megasociety. Even before I arrived in Moscow, my tentative hypothesis was that there probably were plausible parallels, but to that point I had not had the opportunity systematically to test them out. It was only after going through the Soviet experience that I became more confident of the wider implications of the postmodernity hypothesis than I had previously been able to grasp.

What follows is a recapitulation of the substance of the discourses I offered and the dialogue I encountered in Moscow, accompanied by a continuing commentary on the cultural situation to which they were addressed. Chapter one sets the context; chapters two through five report the lecture content and conversation that developed with the undergraduate students of Moscow State University Department of the Scientific and Historical Study of Religion and Freethinking, chapters six and seven summarize lectures and conversations with graduate students, and the last two chapters offer some itinerant social and doxological reflections.

I came to the university under the joint sponsorship of the Humanities Division and the International Institute for Christian Studies. The department chairman, Igor Yablokov, is an affable and wise man who showed warm hospitality to the stranger. Professionally an empirically oriented sociologist of religion, he at several points supplied statistical data that enhanced and sharpened perceptions in the conversation. He sought to keep the dialogue grounded in scientific inquiry, though not in ways that were stifling. His colleagues generously offered me hospitality beyond any deserving, and a quality of dialogue I shall long remember.

I have attempted to describe the transient conditions found in the Soviet Union of February 1991. This does not imply that they might constitute a permanent or durable condition. History is volatile, particularly these days in Soviet culture, and much can change even between the time of writing and publication. But the story seems eminently worth telling, even if ephemeral. Although this effort at description has no specific programmatic or practical political intent, nor does it propose any specific public policy recommendations or resolutions, I cannot help feeling that these analogies have political consequences and moral applications awaiting those better prepared to explore them.

My thesis: The dramatic collapse of Soviet modernity places a telling mirror next to the lingering death of modernity in America. The putrefaction of modernity is oddly similar in these vastly dissimilar systems. A *mod rot* is detectable that penetrates all political barriers and economic histories. The stench permeates our times, east and west. Both societies suffer deeply from analogous forms of social pain. An accurate description of the festering Soviet situation impinges poignantly on the interpretation of prevailing American dilemmas.

PART
ONE

Mod Rot:
The Aroma of Modernity
East and West

CHAPTER
ONE

A Personal Glimpse at Religious Studies in the Soviet University

My visit occurred during the height of the Persian Gulf crisis in the winter of 1991. I left New York for Rome on the very day the air war erupted in earnest. I was in the Soviet Union during the heavy days of the Lithuanian repression, Boris Yeltsin's call for Gorbachev to resign, pro-Yeltsin demonstrations in Moscow, and Soviet diplomatic initiatives to avert the ground war that began just as I was leaving the Soviet Union. The hundred-hour war was just over by the time I returned to New York via Rome.

So, through the February snows of Moscow, I trudged to get

an unusual glimpse of an academic subsystem in transition, and in some respects full reversal. The warmth of the personal hospitality I received in shivering Moscow was captivating and engaging. But why all this for an evangelical scholar, I wondered. I found my hosts more than incidentally interested in the evangelical vitalities remaining within the old-line Protestantism I represented.

The Setting
The lectures were set against the backdrop of a society in decay and an architecture that reeks of totalitarian values. Moscow State University looks like a secularized cathedral, with high spires, classic pillars, baroque marble, and socialist piety exuding everywhere. Built on Stalin's order in massive proportion, the main teaching building itself houses many thousands of students, and is surrounded by a network of auxiliary buildings with huge departmental jurisdictions. From miles away the soaring towers attest the Chartres of Lenin hills. There was measured irony in the voice of the professor who noted that the university building itself was constructed by political prisoners. It still has a kind of prisonlike feel, with military guards at the gates. The military are ubiquitous in Soviet society.

I found the Soviet faculty just as concerned as American faculties about whispered budget cuts. They were earnestly hoping that their vulnerable new experiment in religious studies would not be axed at this imperiled juncture of its reawakening by a retrenching government. All expressed a strong desire to come in closer touch with Western scholars in religious studies. To my surprise, this not only includes but specifically reaches out for classically oriented Christian scholars, and not merely flaky ideologists or exponents of a denuded and barren scientific study of religion. Soviet scholars know enough about the sociology of religion to realize that there is exceptional vitality in American evangelical circles today in contrast to the waning of centerless Protestant liberalism. They are trying to understand these phenomena as intently as we are.

Starved from seven decades of revolutionary gruel amid the Marxist rape of the university, they are now ravenously hungry to discover what has long been happening in religion during their absence. This is a "Rip Van Winkle" moment in Soviet religious studies. They are intensely interested in understanding the last several decades of worldwide theological experience to which they were systematically and brutally denied access.

I found them especially interested in probing questions on how religious faith affects the moral underpinnings of a society and its basic confidence. They were wondering openly how they might appropriate the religious experience of the West in ways that pertain to their current moral, economic and social dilemmas. So the questions they are asking about religion are far from speculative or purely conceptual. They arise out of the tragic depths of their experience of being cut off from free and lively religious discourse for most of this century.

At no time did I feel put down or demeaned. There was no hint of hostility or suspicion. When I sketched the history of my former romanticization of Marxism, and its subsequent disillusionment, and my present belief in the relative justice of the free market where mutual interests are openly negotiated, I expected resistance but got none. They were deeply intrigued by my advocacy of postmodern Christian consciousness. They seemed intently interested in learning what could be reasonably learned from my experience, which had ostensibly been so different from theirs, yet with undercurrents that seemed to them so familiar.

When I described modernity, the collapse of modernity, the emergence of postmodern consciousness, and the vitality of orthodox Christianity within postmodern consciousness, they found the description plausible and an accurate reflection of many analogous aspects of their own experience. Though my life has been spent on the other side of the dismal curtain that divided the world from 1949 to 1989, they quickly recognized that what I had suffered in the failure of modern consciousness was what they had suffered seventy times over and with fiery vengeance.

They are not yet as involved as I in the deliberate textual study of patristic and classical Christian learning, but are intensely curious that this is my vocation. They felt especially drawn to this evangelical-patristic vocation because it gave them a point of contact between vital postmodern Western consciousness and the writings of the Eastern church fathers, who have formed the deep center of consciousness of a thousand years of Russian religious experience.

New Faces among Old Comrades

In the tenth-floor corner room in which the faculty seminar was held, beside the tea and pastries, there was a large glass-cased bookshelf with all the faculty writings in it. The faculty are justifiably proud of their impressive scholarly productivity—fifty or more books and numerous articles that stand as the results of the scholarly efforts of that small departmental faculty. A dozen educators met with me in our initial faculty seminar, with a half dozen others ducking in and out, seeking now and then to answer students' questions, responding to urgent notes and telephone calls.

Though older faculty members may have once been leading

apologists of atheism, most are now hearty advocates of openness in the dialogue about various religious traditions and their social consequences. Various specialists in the department were drawn to issues of the history of religions, church-state relations, political ethics, psychology of religion, and to my surprise, contemporary theology—not only Orthodox but also Catholic and Protestant theological method and dogmatics. While American secular university departments of religion are busy disavowing theology, ironically Soviet studies in religion are intensely intrigued by theology proper: theological method, dogmatics, and the history of Christian doctrine.

I met specialists in the history of atheism, in Russian Orthodoxy, and in contemporary Catholic theology. One professor had written his dissertation on the theological method of Bernard Lonergan, the Canadian Jesuit theologian, had translated the process philosopher Alfred North Whitehead into Russian, and was currently working on an anthology of Western methodological approaches to the study of religion. A social ethicist showed me a monograph he had written on the social essence of Methodism. Once, when I had paraphrased John 1:1-3, assuming I was introducing a new motif into the discussion, to my complete surprise Professor K. I. Nikonov cited in Greek the exact quotation, then outlined a thoughtful exegesis of the Greek text from memory.

One purpose of my visit was to try to assess accurately the status and dynamics of current apologetics for official Soviet atheism. I learned that the university's leading expert on atheism, and the only one in the department still actively engaged in atheistic apologetics, was experiencing a midlife glasnost crisis. Having published several books on atheism that had enjoyed a wide readership in an earlier period, she was now having unexpected difficulty finding a publisher for her writings. When I asked why, the answer was that so few are now interested in atheism. No longer an officially supported state ideology, atheism feels like a ghost of an issue.

They particularly wanted to discuss what methods of inquiry guided our investigations of religion in American universities. They asked especially about the Drew University Ph.D. program in psychology and religion, how it studied both contemporary psychological literature and the ancient tradition of soul care. I described a seminar in which students first read ancient Greek psychology (Plato, Aristotle, Plotinus), then classic early Christian psychology (Anthony, John Chrysostom, Nemesius, Augustine, Gregory the Great), then some medieval and Reformation psychology (Thomas Aquinas, Luther, Calvin, and Richard Baxter), and only then enter into dialogue with modern psychology (in the traditions following Kierkegaard, Pavlov, Wundt, James, Freud, and Jung). Their minds seemed to radiate analogies correlated with their situation.

Since "scientific and historical" appears in their new departmental name, I tried to convey to them something of the crisis that exists in scientific method and historical criticism within American universities. I argued that the critique of criticism was already well underway, especially in the case of biblical historical criticism with the writings of Roland Frye, Martin Hengel, Peter Stuhlmacher, Gerhard Maier, Eta Linnemann, Walter Wink, and others.

When Soviet religion professors speak of the scientific study of religion, they mean a "scientific" frame of reference in which "science" is still strongly shaped by idiosyncratic Soviet intellectual assumptions. I would describe them as former Marxists still studying religion with categories shaped by Leninist premises—

theories they are now honestly trying to reach beyond. It is my guess that none of the people I met at Moscow State University would view themselves as Christian believers in an explicit sense, but they almost all are intensely interested in Christian belief, and emotively drawn toward it—despite their previous involvements with official atheism.

They are afraid that the West will grow weary and disheartened with enigmatic Soviet intransigencies. One professor said he viewed the West as the wellspring of virtually every major reform the Soviets have seen. Another said to me that if the West becomes bored with Soviet immobilism and turns its back on conditions there, things would deteriorate much more quickly, and this would open the door for new repressions. It led me to think that learning Russian and going to the Soviet Union may become a high calling of young scholars in religious studies.

Uneasy Hopes

There is a deep sense of the loss of the thousand-year-old Russian cultural tradition, and hope that it can be in some sense substantively renewed and reappropriated. There is a pathos-laden mourning not for communism or totalitarianism or a centralized economy, but for an organic, stable social order. I came to the sober conclusion that the present government would find it difficult to maintain power long under these circumstances, and what follows may be far less promising.

The Soviet intellectuals, despite their rhetoric, have a deep nostalgia for stability, like many American intellectuals. They laughed when I described the "Gorby" popularity phenomenon in the West, and joked that the difference between Gorbachev in Moscow and Washington is that in Washington he could be elected.

Amid these conditions, Soviet humor abounds. I was told that the present government plan offers two ways to rebuild the country and reform society: a fantasy way and a realistic way. The first way for the country to improve is for everyone to work hard, joining together in a total effort at *perestroika,* so that each one may contribute to social reconstruction. That is the *fantasy* way. Then there is the *realistic* way: The society will be saved by Martians.

As I listened to the layers of concern in the formation of their questions, I was suddenly stunned by the simple awareness that none of these academics or students had any firsthand experience of the Protestant tradition. Their social horizon simply does not include the Protestant experience, though they remain intrigued by it intellectually. I tried to indicate to them that after four centuries of Protestant consciousness, our questions have become thoroughly saturated with Protestant assumptions, even if by way of rejection or neglect. This vast Protestant historical experience is as entirely missing from their intellectual horizon as Stalinism is from mine. They had read Max Weber and R. H. Tawney and understood that the Protestant work ethic affects individual initiative and the formation of capital, but the inner dynamic of how that happens seemed to be a mystery to them.

Having moved from one (czarist) centralized hierarchical order to another (Soviet) centralized hierarchical order, their intellectual tradition had skipped over the entire period from Luther to Wesley, except to borrow from some of the worst rhetoric of Enlightenment skepticism. Their historical consciousness only awakens with the Enlightenment critique of Christianity, not with the Christian underpinnings of the Enlightenment.

I could not help but reflect on the ironies of the relation between the old premodern order and modern deteriorating secular totalitarian order. The old ecclesiastical order has against all odds survived, albeit in bruised and battered form. The modern Soviet order is struggling desperately against disintegration and massive disrepair. Meanwhile Soviet youth seem determined to experiment with the risky edges of what they think is emerging modern consciousness, but which actually is the deteriorating carcass of Enlightenment rationalism: autonomous individualism, narcissistic hedonism, and sexual assertiveness.

Whether *Perestroika* Is Reversible

"Perestroika" is a play on words meaning the unsettling of a former stability. In Brezhnevian days, order and permanence were idealized. With Gorbachev, stability became a code word for undesirable immobility, something to be transcended with better rational constructs. So there is a strong component of Enlightenment idealistic rationalism (as opposed to organic, conserving historical development) in his approach. *Perestroika* is viewed as the calculated destabilizing of the older order and its stability. The high social price of destabilization is beginning to be felt by ordinary Soviet citizens. They yearn for the good old days of relative stability, though not for their police repressions. They are upset that so much that was reliable in the passing order has been so quickly and irretrievably destroyed without being replaced with viable alternatives, only words.

This unhappy patricide, I thought quietly, has been precisely the driving desire of revolutionary thinking and modern chauvinism since the French Revolution. It was easier for that revolution to kill priests than reshape a viable new priesthood. Destroying long-nurtured social structures seems to be what modernity has been best at.

Some of the religion faculty expressed to me their distress that the emerging Soviet leadership would once again be too quick to destroy the recent past. The new political elites, like the old, are prone to be too ready to imagine themselves competent to refashion instantly the conditions for absolute social justice. My hunch is that this is exactly the price that has repeatedly been paid for modern chauvinism since the French Revolution, which invested unchecked power in a supposedly rational vision of the social good only to end in tyranny and destruction. What is happening in Soviet society today risks reverting to the brutal rationalistic idealism of Robespierre. This is why Americans had best not expect a quick or complete reversal of totalitarianism in the Soviet Union, however grateful we may be to Gorbachev for temporarily reducing the power and reach of Soviet military imperialism.

The Soviets astonished me in their intense unhappiness with the early results of *perestroika*, which has rightly sought reforms but not at a prudent pace, and has allowed idealist hopes to take the imagination captive without any consumer payoff. Meanwhile the massive Soviet bureaucracy remains intact. It must be gradually pried loose from its privileges. How to do this gracefully and with determination is a massive, yet delicate leadership task.

It is political folly to try to change society either too quickly or too slowly. Political wisdom seeks to reshape society at that precise pace permitted and required by the contours and limits of a given historical situation, neither slower nor faster. The Soviet problem has long been that change has been either too abrupt or too sluggish. The Soviet leadership does not yet seem to have gained that sort of duly paced wisdom. This period, they said, may be remembered as the period of anarchy in Soviet history. What Soviets feel as already anarchic, however, feels to Americans a little too orderly and immobile. Soviet citizens are quite unaccustomed to seeing on television the kind of challenge that Yeltsin threw to Gorbachev while I was there, when he flatly called for his resignation. Some spoke of possible civil war, which sent shivers down my spine.

The pathos of the present conflict was symbolized for me in a single poignant moment as we walked through the huge metro station near Red Square. There was a romantic-revolutionary statue of a man with pistol, excitedly proclaiming the ideals of the Revolution. My host pointed quietly to the bronze pistol as we passed, shrugged sadly and sighed. There remains a haunting fear of another revolution. The yearning for stability does not imply a desire for political immobilism, but some form of ordered, incremental change.

"Rapid social change," a term we heard so often in the 1960s, saturating the spirit of Vatican II *aggiornamento* and the ethos of the World Council of Churches, I heard repeatedly in Moscow— but with a tired, demoralized accent. There is a visceral revulsion against the ideals of excessively rapid forms of social change that lack political wisdom and organic social continuity. If the West still suffers from the rationalistic revolutionary idealism of the French Revolution, so does Soviet society even more.

Is glasnost irreversible? Here we must appeal less to scientific observation than Christian teaching. All things in history created by human pride, folly, finitude, and imagination are finally reversible, however stable they may at times look. This vulnerability is borne out by the history of seemingly irreversible structures from Byzantium to the Berlin Wall. If anything ever looked irreversible it was Stalinism. By now we should have learned that any claim of irreversibility risks pretense and idolatry. But practically speaking under present historical circumstances, it would be exceedingly difficult to reverse glasnost, even with a vast police apparatus.

My last lecture ended on a personal note. I spoke about my daughter who had walked from Leningrad to Moscow in 1987 on behalf of peace and the person-to-person meeting of Russians and Americans during the cold war. Having studied the Russian language and literature in college, she felt called to organize the first peacewalk of 230 Americans in the Soviet Union. Passing around her picture, "oohh-ing" and "ahhh-ing," they realized instinctively that some Americans really care about them and are willing to go out of their way to show love and concern for the Soviet people. The session ended not with any further comment on my lecture but with the department chairman expressing how grateful they were to Laura. Her act of self-giving seemed far more important than anything I had said.

I left the university clutching a bundle of letters that professors gave me to mail in the United States. When I indicated that I would not return to the US until a week later, they laughed: "What's a week in relation to our postal system? All we want is to be assured *that* they will be mailed, not *when*."

CHAPTER TWO

Postmodern Consciousness

My first purpose is to define modernity, then postmodernity. Then in the next chapter I will define Christian consciousness within postmodernity. These definitions strike me as indispensably pertinent to the description of both Soviet and American historical situations. It is necessary to grasp this situation accurately if the dialog between us is to proceed realistically. Only then can we speak meaningfully of methods of inquiry into religion.

An Epoch, an Ideology and a Malady
Modernity is best defined first as a historical period, then as an

ideological worldview, and finally as a malaise of the deteriorating phase of that worldview.

1. The duration of the *epoch* of modernity is now clearly identifiable as a precise two-hundred-year period between 1789 and 1989, between the French Revolution and the collapse of communism. Such dating of historical periods is always disputable, but this one cries out with clarity, since it was announced with such a dramatic beginning point (the storming of the Bastille), and closed with such a precise moment of collapse (the literal fall of a vast symbolic concrete wall in Berlin). The analogies between the revolutions of 1789 and 1989 will intrigue historians for centuries to come.

2. Within the bounds of these two centuries, an *ideological worldview* has arisen and fallen, come and gone. This worldview is filled with the humanistic ethics and scientific values and idealistic hopes of the Enlightenment period. These ideas have dominated modern times. This worldview has promoted—within the modern university, media, and church—the assumptions, values, and ideology of the French Enlightenment, coupled with German idealism and British empiricism. These ideas have invaded and to some degree temporarily conquered university communities, including those founded by Protestant and Catholic educators.

By the way, "modernism" is not exactly what I mean by modernity. Modernism a term used within Catholic and Protestant theology for a particular set of movements within modernity which commend the values of the modern ideological worldview. I prefer to distinguish the broader term modernity from the narrower term modernism, which it encompasses.

3. Finally, modernity is a languishing social *malady* within this worldview, in both East and West. That worldview has been spiraling downward in a relentless disarray during the three dec-

ades from 1960 to 1990, the period of rapidly deteriorating modernity. The malaise is acute in the American setting and chronic in the Soviet setting.

Four Motifs of Decadent Modernity

Modernity is epitomized by the reductive naturalism of Freud which is no longer viable as a therapy, the historical utopianism of Marx which is now in a cynical phase of collapse from Vilnius to Managua, the narcissistic assertiveness of Nietzsche which is now killing itself on Los Angeles streets, and the modern chauvinism of Strauss, Troeltsch and Bultmann which exalts the ethos of late modernity itself to a norm that judges all premodern texts and ideas.

These four motifs flow together into an ethos that still sentimentally shapes the knowledge elites of American universities, who remain largely unprepared to grasp fully their own vulnerability within this historical situation. They are behind the curve, following the wave, and not up to the speed of the actual reversals of contemporary history. They are still mourning the Nicaragua election, the defeat of ERA, and fantastic success of the market exchange. The knowledge elites (media, academics, bureaucrats) are tardy in grasping the moral insights that have long since been grasped by the longsuffering voters, taxpayers, and general working populace.

There are four key motifs of modernity that are in a process of collapse, each now hammering out the final paragraphs of its own epitaph:

1. *Autonomous individualism* focuses on the detached individual as a self-sufficient, sovereign self. This individualism is in crisis today. Western societies are now having to learn to live with the consequences of the social destruction to which excessive indi-

vidualism has led the "me-first-now" generation. The curtain
closes with the whimpering sighs of the me generation, whose
progeny are being forced to become the "us" generation.

2. *Narcissistic hedonism* is in crisis today. It is best symbolized by
the recent history of sexuality. The party is over for the sexual
revolution. The party-crasher and terminator is AIDS. We are
now having to learn to live with the consequences of the sexual
and familial devastation to which hedonism has led us. It is visible
in living color whenever one turns on the television tube for
what is called "entertainment," which turns out to be fixated on
sex and violence. The social fruits of hedonism are loneliness,
divorce, and the substitution of sexual experimentation for intimacy.

By narcissism, I mean the excessive love of one's own comfort
and importance. Remember that Echo in Greek mythology was
a nymph who, for the love of Narcissus, pined away until nothing remained of her but her voice. Nemesis punished Narcissus
by causing him to pine away for love of his own reflection in a
spring, and changed him into a daffodil. The gaze of a narcissistic
generation is fixed primarily upon itself in constant self-involve-
ment and self-congratulation. The way narcissism translates into
historical perspective is modern chauvinism, which assumes that
we moderns are better than all previous thinkers, and whose
footnotes are only recent sources which always turn out to be
morally superior to anything that went before.

A key indicator of the excesses of modern narcissism is compulsive drug usage accompanied by sexual experimentation, all to
achieve artificial momentary highs or supposed peak experiences,
even at the known cost of unwanted pregnancies and suffering
children. That one's narcissistic binge is another's lifelong misery
is evident from the fact that last year in our country 375,000

children were born suffering from their mothers' drug addictions.

3. *Reductive naturalism* is that view that reduces all forms of knowing to laboratory experimentation, empirical observation or quantitative analysis. It is the reduction of sex to orgasm, persons to bodies, psychology to stimuli, economics to planning mechanisms, and politics to machinery.

Reduction is an act of diminishing in scope, value or force. To reduce is to bring into a lesser state, diminish, impoverish. In this case we are talking about the attempted reduction of creation to nature, of all causality to natural causality, of replete experience to gaunt empirical explanation. We are now being forced to learn to live with and beyond the melancholy consequences of this emaciated, skeletal approach to truth. This ideology of diminution is today in crisis.

4. *Absolute moral relativism* views all moral values as merely relative to the changing, processing determinants of human cultures. It is dogmatically absolute in its moral relativism because it asserts that relativism uncritically.

This leaves no room to ask about that One in relation to whom all relativities are themselves relative. It is to this One that Jews and Christians have prayed, and upon whom their best minds have reflected for millennia—the infinite One in relation to whom all finite relativities are relative.

Absolute moral relativism is everywhere today in crisis, as seen comically in the condom dispute in American education and tragically in the hospital wards filled with crack babies. In the postmodern world we have been forced to live with the disastrous social results of absolute moral relativism—the forgetfulness of final judgment beyond history, the reduction of all moral claims to a common denominator of mediocrity. Our communities have suffered deeply from the pretense that all value judgments are equally legitimate and all ideas equally tolerable, since presumed to be exhaustively formed by social determinants, and without any transcendent reference. We are now having to learn to live beyond the moral anomie into which this modern dogmatism has plunged us.

Marx, Nietzsche, Freud and Bultmann

These cardinal motifs are epitomized in four key figures who have led the way into the final stages of this crisis. Four types of criticism, which formerly were dominant, having held sway in modernity, are now struggling with social failure at every hand: Nietzschean relativistic nihilism, Marxist social planning, Freudian therapy, and Bultmannian historicism.

1. Briefly, Friedrich Nietzsche furnished modernity with the sharp knife of a cynical, egoistic critique of all moral striving. The view that religion is an expression of personal weakness, and that egoistic self-assertiveness is the most blessed possible human condition—this is the toxic heritage Nietzsche left behind, and which has come to characterize the late stages of modernity.

2. Karl Marx offered a class location critique which assumed that every ideological view has its final explanation in one's position in the class struggle. He viewed religion as forever captive to economic interests, and reducible to them.

Meanwhile the Marxist regulators and planners who thought they were able rationally to provide a more just instrument than the free exchange of market interests have proven to be just as self-interested as the market. They have become demonic mentors to vulnerable idealists more attracted to ideas than actual history or real people.

Modernity has had enough of Marx. Nowhere is the end of

modern economic rationalism more clear than in countries like the Soviet Union, which have long suffered from command economies and a repressive police apparatus.

3. Sigmund Freud offered modernity a psychoanalytic critique which imagined that all neurotic behavior is grounded in sexual repression. "Whatever became of sin?" is the haunting sermon song of Karl Menninger that symbolizes the denouement of this critique. The view that morality and religion are expressions of neurotic sexual fixations is the bizarre heritage of Freudianism, which has too often left its path strewn with broken human and familial relationships.

4. The last representative figure could just as easily be David Friedrich Strauss or Ernst Troeltsch as Rudolf Bultmann. But since Bultmann is of more recent vintage and more familiar, we choose him as the epitome of that modern chauvinism which assumes that recent worldviews are intrinsically superior to ancient ones.

Bultmann gave us a way of investigating the oral traditions behind the texts: form criticism. Bultmannianism is based upon a Heideggerian analysis of human existence which reduces all speech about God to statements about human being-in-the-world. The salvation event is viewed more as a memory in the minds of struggling, despairing rememberers than an actual historical event. The conversion of religious studies into a speculative ideology of reductive historicism is the toxic residue Bultmann left behind. These have long been standard working hypotheses for an aging guild of New Testament scholars.

Much more could be said in favor of Marx, Nietzsche, Freud and Bultmann, and such thumbnail sketches are only partial impressions. But the function of caricature is to capture something crucial about the contours of a face, while leaving out much detail. While each of the above descriptions is admittedly an incomplete portrait, each is pathetically true in essence.

It is difficult to deny the toxicity of the results of these four figures, even when one is keenly aware of their other considerable exploits and achievements, which I personally have documented and lauded in my earlier writings. As an autobiographical aside, those who know me well will already recognize that I have been strongly affected by all of these voices in my trek through modernity. Bultmann, for example, brought the New Testament alive to me as a youthful skeptic. Long after I had written my Yale dissertation on Bultmann and Barth, my heart had remained Bultmannian. As late as the mid-sixties, I was writing in defense of a restrained Bultmannian position, defending him against Ogden and Buri on the left and Schniewind and Thielicke on the right. So I do not enter this discussion as one attacking from the outside, but a once-friendly mole who has surfaced from the inside after a long experience of disaffection.

Our Times: The Death Bed of Modernity
Each of these key modern modes of inquiry is now in deep anguish and distress. The more pathetic, lingering "death bed" metaphor seems more accurate than the flattering metaphor of a completed death. Modernity east and west is in its final crisis of waning strength, but could linger for some time.

1. Freudian psychoanalysis is in its final stages of hegemony. It is being generally repudiated as a mode of therapy and scientific anthropology. Freud has taught us to investigate the unconscious motivations of action, but the bad faith of psychoanalysis itself is now being investigated. The methods of psychoanalysis are ineffective. The spontaneous remission rate (recovery without therapeutic intervention), about 62 per cent, is as good as or

better than the rate of recovery under psychoanalysis.

2. Bultmannian historicism, while still struggling to maintain the semblance of its former influence among Protestant theological faculties, is now largely being discarded because of its speculative nature, limited anthropology, and oversimplified idealization of "modern man."

3. The house of cards of Marxism came tumbling down with the fall of the Berlin Wall, and of faltering control economies throughout Eastern Europe. I do not want to speculate on the future of Marxist ideology, but it seems evident that the suffering of seventy years will not be mended by intensifying police state totalitarianism.

What caused it to collapse so quickly? The rapidity of its demise is partly explained by the fact that it had promised so much for so long with such little result. Promise making eventually requires promise keeping. The fury of promises unkept has swept away the former apparent security of the Marxist world. Once the despot shows the slightest vulnerability, all is lost.

4. Nietzschean self-assertiveness has entered into a rapidly deteriorating phase. Those who have attempted to live it out have found that its nihilism and egoism can only take one a short distance toward the building of viable human families and communities. Radical lesbian feminism is the best example of the deadly consequences of Nietzschean assertiveness, especially when combined with post-Freudian forms of fantasized freedom from social constraint.

Radical feminism, which had earlier focused on the legitimate rights of women to human dignity and fair treatment, has ended by becoming preoccupied with cynical individual self-assertiveness. It has in the long run tended to undermine human community, outfox sexual intimacy, and subvert covenant sexual commitment. A strong case can be made that feminism itself is in significant ways responsible for the feminization of poverty, by its insistence on the independent identity of women, by its idealization of women with children without men, and by public policies that have encouraged divorce, increased the vulnerability of families, and left women to their own devices. Feminism has turned into a binge of egocentricity, but it is largely over. We are now picking up the pieces. The apex year of feminist influence was 1984, the year of the nomination of Geraldine Ferraro and the defeat of ERA.

Undifferentiated unisex fantasies and repressive egalitarian dreams are collapsing as postfeminist writers like Midge Dechter, Sylvia Ann Hewlett, Sarah Blaffer Hrdy, Eleanore Stump, Connie Marshner and Nicholas Davidson are finally exploding the myths of absolute, abstract sexual egalitarianism. Women are uniquely capable of virtues which men find it harder to develop, even as men are capable of virtues women find harder to nurture. Women have played key roles in modern history, but seldom according to the nostalgic radical chic feminist premises so dear to liberal bureaucrats and media aristocracy. Imaginative women like Mother Teresa, Margaret Thatcher and Phyllis Schlafly do not fit into any category system available to prevailing knowledge elitists.

What Is Left?

We are now entering into a historical phase in which modernity is dying, and whatever is to follow modernity is already taking embryonic shape. No one can any longer pretend that these deteriorating forces have vitality except among certain protected elites, in some universities, some church circles, and some bureaucracies.

No one who is aware of public opinion analysis can any longer assert the hegemony of these modern assumptions in emerging historical consciousness. The Marxist-Leninism of the Soviet period, the Freudian sexual liberation of the American culture, the Nietzscheanism of European nihilism, and the modern chauvinism of Bultmann are all deteriorating social processes, each now unmasked as having a limited vision of human history and possibility. All are under siege. They are now falling like dominoes. Each has colluded to support the other. They are modern conceptualities that are having enormous difficulties dragging themselves into the postmodern world. All four are quintessentially modern, not postmodern.

How far along are we into the demise of modernity and the birth of postmodernity? I am trying to describe a long developing, fundamental social process and crisis of consciousness of which no one can foresee the result. The transition may last many decades. Now we see only a deepening crisis. But out of it by grace may come a society no longer satisfied with the demoralizing assumptions of modernity. For those who have eyes to see, we are already through the ideological funeral of the four key assumptions of modernity, although it may take time to realize just how unresponsive are the corpses. The funeral occurred in 1989.

Postmodernity

If these are echoes of the modern agony, what is meant by postmodernity? While modernity is dying, what exactly is the thing being born?

History does not stand still. It is always confronting us with new constraints, options and requirements. The challenge today is not the same as in 1917 or 1945 or 1968, and there is no profit in redoing those revolutions. How can the present challenge be described?

Although we are at the end of modernity, there no cause for despair, apocalyptic anxiety or pointless frustration. We are being invited to remain open precisely to these new historical conditions, and see these very deteriorations as offering the promise of a vital new expression of providential possibility. Biblically viewed, this dissolution is a providential judgment of sin and an opportunity for convicting grace. Christians believe that amid any cultural death, new gifts of the providential guidance of God are being offered to humanity, and unsullied forms of the providential hedging of God in history are emerging so as to curb human folly and sin.

I remain temperamentally a modern man in many ways, even amid modernity's collapse. I can continue to appreciate many technological and some social and economic achievements of modernity, as I soberly recognize that their ideological underpinnings are now in radical crisis.

It should be evident that I do not mean by postmodernity what Derrida and Foucault mean or say about deconstructionism. The unhappy campers that follow Derrida apply the hermeneutic of suspicion to each premise or assertion. They are not postmodern but ultramodern. In another sense they are reactionary, in that they are reverting once again to the radical skepticism of the Enlightenment. They represent a phase of modernity in its death throes that is trying to locate some edge of plausibility in the dying assumptions of modernity. Deconstructionism has about it the smell of death. It will not last more than a decade, or among unfeigned believers a generation. Jews and Christians have been through these fits of skepticism many times before. The transition from modernity to postmodernity may take many decades, but it has definitely already begun.

Some of my friends are annoyed with me that I have remained stubbornly determined to use the term postmodern in my own reclusive way, with a meaning far different from recent pop deconstructionists'. I delight in pointing out to them that I was writing about postmodernity precisely this way in 1968, when Rorty was unsung, long before the deluge of deconstructionism. I invite them to supply reasons why I should change my usage merely to fit the pattern of others who are more recently corrupting the term as a euphemism for ultramodernity.

The Promise of the Postmodern Future

The second millennium is ending with the demise of modernity. The world after the end of the second millennium will necessarily be constructed on the foundations of the old.

This turn, this reversal of consciousness, suggests that we are now living in a fecund, volatile, decisive and potentially pivotal period of historical change. New human alternatives are suddenly viable, possiblities which no one could have foreseen only a short time ago. We need not be driven to despair or frustration by the pressures these possibilities bring upon us.

Postmodern consciousness is formally defined simply as that form of consciousness that necessarily must follow the era of modernity (the *period* from 1789 to 1989 which characteristically espoused an Enlightenment *worldview* which is now in *malaise*). If one takes the premise that the modernity we have described is lurching toward death, and that history will continue, whatever it is that will continue will be postmodernity. If X is ending, then post-X is emerging. If what is ending is called modernity, then what is to follow we call postmodernity. It is not a program but a succession. "Post" is the Latin prefix meaning simply after or following upon or later than. So postmodernity in my meaning is nothing more or less complicated than *what follows modernity*.

The freedom and finitude of humanity, in all its glory and despair, will play in unpredictable ways into the postmodern future. All we can be reasonably sure of is that it is not likely to not be a rerun of modernity.

What is postmodern consciousness beginning to look like? Since no one can see into the future, it would be folly to pretend to make a program out of futurity. Those who describe the present situation and then pretend to extrapolate these trends indefinitely do not understand the reversibility of human freedom. It is always possible to revert to the habits of modernity, even though it is hard to imagine anyone foolish enough to try now to resurrect Freud or Marx or Nietzsche after having suffered so deeply from them. Those who attach to postmodernity a fixed trajectory, platform or definite program are still caught up in modern fantasies of determinism and inevitable optimism.

Given these limits, it is still possible to ponder the directions we will likely be struggling toward in the postmodern decades ahead. In my view, we will more likely be searching for incremental shifts toward proximate justice rather than pretentious massive shifts that invite revolutionary rhetoric. We will more likely be seeking organic changes grounded in particular rooted social traditions, than planning on the pretense that no previous history or neighborhoods or families ever existed. We will more likely be investing confidence in smaller, more local political units rather than always looking to empires and bureaucratic schemes to resolve Main Street's domestic problems. We will be asking localities to take responsibility for their own futures rather than turn their futures over to planners who will always plan their own interest first in any social design. We will be searching for the peaceful negotiation of conflicting interests, with a strong determination to resist flagrant aggression where necessary. We will be searching for fair mechanisms that will allow free markets to work without inordinate protectionism and tariffs and political constraints, so that producers and distributors of goods and services may make their own judgments about their own interests in economic exchange.

Above all, postmodern consciousness will be searching for the recovery of the family, for enduring marriages and good environments for the growth and nurture of children. Postmodernity whether East or West will be searching for a way back to the eternal verities that grounded society before the devastations of late modernity. The direction of postmodernity, in short, promises to be an organic approach to incremental change grounded in traditionally tested values. It will nurture the incremental increase of slow-growing human organisms and friendships and sexual fidelity more than the rhetoric of massive social change.

That is what I think will happen in the postmodern world. But it will happen more out of necessity and revulsion than as a result of some vast, new and rationalistic human blueprint on some planner's desk. Meanwhile the emerging world will once again appear to nostalgic apologists of modernity like a reactionary rehearsal of an old tune. Anyway, who are we—poor infirm finite creatures—to guess the future? The only thing certain about the future is that it will outlive our predictions.

What remains good and lasting and redeemable about modernity? Each attempted answer points to some ambiguous, vulnerable, corruptible and finite good, not to any consummate or unconditional good: democratic capitalism, technological achievement, rapid transport, computer technology, flushing toilets, neon cities that buzz and dance with frenetic market exchange,

medical breakthroughs, photocopy machines, portable telephones, plastic credit cards, braking systems, biogenetics, the
blues, the steel guitar, Dr. Scholl's foot powder, Dr. Spock's advice, and Dr. K's screwball. This is all modernity, and who would
dare claim that it is either all bad or all gone? But whether it can
save from sin, or render life meaningful, or heal guilt or relieve
anxiety or liberate from idolatry—here we must not claim too
much. With each modern technological achievement come com-
pounded temptations to treat that limited good as if absolute, and
to use good means for evil ends.

The Leaky Condom

I choose the condom as the quintessential symbol of leaking modernity. No technological artifice better tells the story of autonomous individualism, narcissistic hedonism and reductive naturalism than this flimsy rubber sheath which is said to be 80%
"effective" with educated use.

What is a condom? Third graders know. Its primary intention
is to prevent human life. Often it "succeeds." When it doesn't,
it "fails." Those who zealously count on it risk feeling disappoint-
ed, baffled and betrayed. Its secondary intent is to prevent disease, yet in the era of its widest use there is runaway incidence
of syphilis, gonorrhea, chlamydia and the various herpes viruses.

The world is now divided into two parts: Those who think
"safe sex" condoms tend on the whole to improve, enhance and
ennoble the human future, and those convinced that condoms do
not make promiscuous sex any safer. Vast school systems are
divided into two parts: Those who urge teaching small children
to use condoms and those who think that is unconscionable. This
is the exact line of demarcation between modernity and postmodernity.

In 1968, Paul VI issued a controversial encyclical, *Humanae Vitae*, in which artificial birth control was reproved as an unnatural intrusion into the right ordering of human sexuality. After two decades of assuming that this encyclical was the height of naiveté and indiscretion, and after living through the consequences of a retrogressive period of sexual immoderation, some of us can only wonder about the extraordinary social prescience of this curious instruction. Might it have been more suitable to family blessedness, after all? Though this is a question few Protestants are yet willing to ask, more may become willing if the consequences of sexually transmitted diseases continue to pile up in our disfavor.

To reassure some who might otherwise be worried about my sanity, I am not suggesting that the invention of the condom is a work of the devil or that family planning strategies of all sorts have no place whatever in our sexual future. But there seems little reason to trust that the condom will be the great rubber hope for the conquering of sexually transmitted disease. The answer to sexually transmitted disease is more a moral and volitional than a technological solution. The way is narrow that leads to covenant fidelity and enduring intimacy. There is no technological fix to ensure the cohesion of the family.

There are some runner-up candidate symbols of the joint ironic success and failure of modernity—maybe the hypodermic needle, Valium, smart bombs, the microchip, *Hustler*, chlorofluorocarbons and DDT. But none says more about what modernity promises and delivers than the leak-prone condom.

Christian
Perseverance
After Modernity

When my students at Drew asked me what I was going to say in
Moscow, I answered that I did not precisely know, but
would first have to listen to the voices and behold the
faces of Moscow before I could sense what might be appropriate
to say there. Even when I had only been in the Soviet Union a
short time, I found that my perspectives were already being re-
shaped by their concerns and sculpted by their circumstances.
What follows reflects a preliminary reading from that different
angle of vision.

Two Worlds

As I listened and spoke in Moscow, I felt myself living between two worlds. I was seeking to translate the perceptions and codices of one accurately to the other. I loved and esteemed and respected both, and felt myself a part of both.

But which two worlds? East and West seemed an inadequate geographical metaphor that did not reach the depth of the contrast. Communist and capitalist did not any longer adequately describe the real differences.

Which worlds was I trying to embrace and reconcile in Moscow, so as to facilitate communication? I realized that they must be described not only spatially or geographically but temporally, not only East and West, but modern and postmodern. Both worlds are found in both East and West, yet with different histories with distinct memories. Christianity inhabits both worlds. To describe accurately these two worlds is what I want to try to do. I tried to schematize it as in figure 3.1.

The metaphor of two worlds, therefore, has the double entendre of both East/West and modern/postmodern. What might we learn from such a picture, which admittedly is a visual paraphrase? As far as east is from west, so modernity is morose wherever we turn, imparting its annoying aroma of *mod rot*. Meanwhile postmodern consciousness is emerging across all previously assumed impenetrable barriers of economic and political systems. Pilgrim orthodoxy is rediscovering its identity amid this postmodern passage.

Orthodoxy Remembers Many Former Modernities
Jewish and Christian believers have been through many modernities. This is not the first or only one.

In the late medieval period emerged a *via moderna*, a once-new "modern way" of nominalism, that stood as a powerful challenge to medieval scholasticism (which only two centuries earlier had

The Two Worlds Viewed as Geographic Place	Eastern World	Western World	The Two Worlds Viewed as Time (reading downward)
Premodernity:	Eastern Orthodoxy	Catholic and Protestant Orthodoxy	
Early Modernity: Grounded in:	Czarist Modernization French Enlightenment	Enlightenment Rationalism British Empiricism & German Idealism	Modern World 1789-1989
Late Modernity: Embodied in:	Eastern Bloc of Cold War Soviet Atheism	Western Bloc of Cold War European-American Secularization	
Epitomized by:	Marx	Nietzsche Freud Strauss	
	Totalitarian Communism	Democratic Capitalism	
	Autonomous Collectivism	Autonomous Individualism	
Then Came 1989 * * * * * * * Postmodern Christian Future:	1989 * * * * * * Postatheistic Orthodoxy	1989 * * * * * * Postmodern Orthodoxy	1989 * * * * * * Postmodern World
The Required Healing:	Recovery from Absolutist Communism	Recovery from Absolutist Individualism	
Urgent Social Tasks:	Marketing Voting Worshiping	Parenting Conserving Traditioning	

itself been a novel and imaginative undertaking). This late medieval modernity was a theory of knowledge which insisted that universals are concepts created by reason, that essences have no independent reality of their own but are only names, that all universal or abstract terms are conveniences of language, and therefore exist as labels only and have no realities corresponding to them. In this way, reality was denied to universal concepts, as opposed to realism. That *via moderna* contributed to the general skepticism of the age preceding the Reformation. Historic Christianity wrestled with that modernity, sorted out its legitimate and illegitimate features, transmuted it, lived beyond it, and watched its death.

Our current and once-proud modernity is also dying. Something else is being born. Those who remember that sin pervades all human striving will not expect postmodern consciousness to be without pride, sensuality, and perennial elements of human absurdity. But we do have a right to expect that we can learn something from the social disasters of recent decades.

Christianity invites the dispossessed, nomadic families of modern times not to be afraid to enter the postmodern world. When we commit our lives to particular forms of idolatrous faith in passing finite structures of historical formation, and when these beloved arrangements and systems die, we understandably grieve and feel angry and frustrated. Meanwhile, Christians celebrate the hidden providence of history, whereby each dying historical formation is giving birth to fresh occasions for responsible human life.

God is present in the death of cultures as destroyer of idols and judge of the sin of past cultures, as of persons. Through death God makes way for ever new personal and cultural formations. Cultures come and go, but God lives from everlasting to everlasting. Human beings see the river of time from a particular vantage point on the bank, but God, as if from above, sees the entire river in its whole extent, at every point, and simultaneously (Hilary, *On the Trinity*, 12).

Postmodern Christians pray that postatheistic Soviets will find the courage to face their own specific postmodern future, caring deeply about the needy neighbor amid the emergence of the new future, and not resenting the inexorable fact that each culture like each person dies.

The Postmodern Rediscovery of Classic Christian Teaching

Christianity gives us power and means of trusting fundamentally in the One who offers us this ever-changing, forever-dying historical process. Even when we and our idolatries are threatened, the ground and giver of history is friendly and eternally forgiving.

\The central feature of Jewish and Christian consciousness in the postmodern situation is the profound rediscovery of the texts of long-ignored classical Jewish and Christian traditions, rabbinic and patristic. For Christians, this means especially the Eastern church fathers of the first five Christian centuries. The methodological fulcrum that began changing this trajectory is attentiveness to the written Word and its most widely received early expositors\

\What is happening amid this historical situation is a return to the sacred texts of the early Christian Scripture and the exegetical guides of the formative period of its canonization and interpretation. Postmodern Christians are those who, having entered in good faith into the disciplines of modernity, and having become disillusioned with the illusions of modernity, are again studying the Word of God made known in history.\It is attested by prophetic and apostolic witnesses whose testimonies, letters and gospels have become canonical texts for this worldwide, multicultural, multigenerational remembering and celebrating community. Those who gave definitive form to the ecumenical interpretation of these texts are the patristic writers, four in the East (Athanasius, Basil, Gregory Nazianzen, and John Chrysostom), and four in the West (Ambrose, Augustine, Jerome, and Gregory the Great).

\It remains possible within the premises of postmodern consciousness to engage in a scientific study of all this religious testimony and experience—pressing for objective, fair-minded inquiry.\By that we do not mean that we disregard the object of inquiry, God. The best way to take that One seriously is to take seriously the historical concretions of consciousness—prayers, sacred texts, liturgies, spiritual disciplines—which have emerged out of the worship of that One.

There is, of course, no single definitive mode of postmodern thinking, and certainly no singular, unchallenged, universally approved approach to Christian postmodern consciousness. We seek to describe an ecumenical rainbow, not a narrow, monolithic, and fixed entity.

The modern/postmodern distinction is too flatly perceived if viewed merely as the general truism that one civilization is dying and another emerging. Few would quarrel with that way of putting it, but it hardly advances the argument. The hard disagreements come in trying to describe what precisely has been passing away, what is coming to be, and how Christian orthodoxy and catholicity relate to both.

Specifically, I mean that a world is dying, perhaps not wholly dead yet, but bereft of vitality, and only awaiting the end of a lingering death. That world is the world dominated by the failed ideas of autonomous individualism, narcissistic hedonism, reductive naturalism, and absolute moral relativism. Others may call that world something other than modernity, but I have no better way of naming it.

In describing the trek from modernity to postmodernity, I am in part describing my own autobiographical journey. After spending at least half of my life as a defender of modernity, what has changed from the old "me" is the steady slow growth toward orthodoxy (consensual ancient classic Christianity), with its proximate continuity, catholicity and apostolicity. This implies a growing resistance to faddism, novelty, heresy, anarchism, antinomianism, pretensions of discontinuity, revolutionary talk and nonhistorical idealism. My old liberal friends think that what is happening to me is just the usual result of ordinary psychogenetic development, which is a polite way of reminding me I am growing quite a bit older, which I am grateful not to have to deny. As a parent, I am personally deeply grateful that our three children have somehow by some mysterious grace negotiated the hazards of tottering modernity without crippling effects, and come out on the other side not battered or shredded as persons.

Whether Postmodernity Finally Amounts to Antimodernity

Postmodern consciousness is not rightly understood merely as a reactionary rejection of all things modern, or a simple negative emotive reaction against modernity. Mark well: There is no reason to be opposed to something that is dead. *Antimodernity makes the egregious error of overestimating the continuing power of modernity.*

Were modernity still full of vitality, the hypothesis would make more sense that what postmodernity really amounts to is merely a furious and frustrated attack upon modernity. The leading observation of postmodern consciousness is not that modernity is bad, but that it is dead\ *This is why postmodern orthodoxy is not rightly defined as antimodern.*

My feeling is less anger than poignancy about the pathos-laden death of modernity. The period of mourning is over for many of us. It lasted long enough, and we have to go on with living.

*Post*modern or *Ultra*modern?

Meanwhile astute readers are advised to strike *post* and insert *ultra* when the word *postmodernity* is used by most academics. For them *postmodern* often means simply *ultramodern*. The word brawl may be schematized as in figure 3.2.

Fluff Posties	Tough Posties
Academic Guild Postmoderns	Religious Postmoderns
Where ultramodern could plausibly substitute for postmodern	Where postmodern refers to what experientially follows the death of modernity
Postmodernity as a hermeneutical theory to be debated, constructed and deconstructed in universities	Postmodernity as an actual experience to be lived, negotiated and survived in presently unfolding history
Exponents: Hagiographers of St. Karl, St. Friedrich and St. Sigmund	Exponents: Neo-Athanasians whose task is modern halo inspection, counter-hagiography

Figure 3.2.   Competing Usages of the Term *Postmodernity*

For fluff posties *postmodern* is a linguistic oxymoron. For hard postmoderns, postmodernity is a frightful historical reality. An oxymoron is a sharp-dull saying which by looking smart says something foolish. Academics are prone to the oxymoronic usage of the term *postmodernity*.

These two meanings are competing in earnest for the single term *postmodern*—whether with a soft or a hard meaning. Traditional Jews and Christians are choosing a harder usage, for the actual world we must live in following the devastations of Enlightenment modernity is a real world of AIDS, dope, gangs, and Madonna, not merely a debatable theory of interpretation grounded in the ideas of Freud, Marx and Nietzsche.

Guild posties are less interested in the actual struggling history of human sufferers following the collapse of modernity than in securing their tenure so they can spin out endless deconstructions. The terrible apocalypse envisioned by orthodox postmodern Christians is already becoming an actual history. Hard postmodernity must now live with the battered world created by the saints of the soft posties.

Jacques Derrida and Richard Rorty have led us into a cult of subjectivism and sentiment that reduces truth to subjective preference and celebrates a new hagiography. There are three leading canonized saints of the passing order: Saint Karl, Saint Friedrich and Saint Sigmund. Richard Rorty is hardly a saint, but does pretend to be a practical user of the gnosis of the saints. Christians know that Rorty and company's day will not be long, but meanwhile human beings are suffering with the consequences of an actual postmodern world spawned by ultramodernity.

In a decisive twist of irony, the very university establishments once spawned by classical Christianity now offer tenured radical chairs to those who debunk Christian saints and promote the ultramodern canon. A central task of their modernist hagiography is the negative task of castigating all previous saints. Amid this scene a language war rages over the most fitting use of the term *postmodern*. It is an Athanasian task that must be pursued *contra mundo*.

Ordinary working people do not suffer much from the prolix buzzings of soft postie theories of interpretation, but they do suffere daily and silently over acutal hard postmodern history. It is this history to which postmodern orthodox Christians must point fearlessly without being intimidated by fluff posties. We are living through an actual period of postmodern grief and reconstruction. For in the real postmodern world we live with the devastating consequences that have followed the ideologies of those whom the post (read *ultra*) modern academics view as saints. While the Enlightenment ideology of Saints Karl, Friedrich and Sigmund are moribund, the children of the world they spawned struggle to survive in single-parent hovels with latchkey kids shaped morally by MTV.

The Postmodern Promise of Paleo-ecumenism
Surprisingly, the rediscovery of ancient ecumenical Christianity opens up a fresh possibility for significant dialogue between Soviet and American university studies in religion. The historical substratum of Russian social consciousness has been deeply and secretly formed by the very patristic writers of the first five centuries only now being rediscovered in the territory west of Geneva and Rome.

Americans are now belatedly finding their way into these ancient Eastern church writers—in addition to those already named, Eusebius, Cyril of Jerusalem, Cyril of Alexandria, Gregory of Nyssa, Ephraim Syrus, John of Damascus—writers long revered in the Orthodox East who have been too long neglected in the Catholic and Protestant West. This opens the door for a new form of interaction between our two societies, especially in the arena of university studies in religion, quite apart from any ecclesial or ecumenical discussions that might or might not pro-

ceed between particular churches and their bureaucratic agents.
There is growing evidence that the rediscovery of the ancient
Christian writers, especially Eastern church fathers, is emerging
as a potential breakthrough concern within contemporary Christian scholarship, including evangelical Protestantism. Please refer
to the bibliography for a list of key books that have been carrying
forth this task, and for a list of continuing series of primary
patristic sources and translations published since 1950. These
bibliographies represent a major late twentieth century revitalization of patristic studies that is not confined to Roman Catholic
and Eastern Orthodox writers, but is also being strongly influenced by bright evangelical Protestant voices such as those of
Robert Webber, Donald Bloesch, Frederick Dale Brunner, and
Frederick W. Norris. Happily, paleo-ecumenical inquiry does not
have to await the strange dance of bureaucrats negotiating and
posturing for ecumenical agreements.

Hence there appears to be an unexpected coalescence of interests between Soviet and American approaches to the study of
religion which in their recent histories have been so dissimilar.
The renewal of the study of patristic sources brings the American tradition suddenly closer to the Eastern tradition, and thus
inevitably closer to the Russian tradition and its related Slavic
variations. This long-postponed inquiry is as inviting to postliberal Americans as it is to postatheistic Soviets. It offers a transProtestant and postmodern basis upon which the future of religious dialog might proceed in our two diverse societies. This
opens up a new avenue of dialog reaching across the gutted
barriers of what used to be the cold war.

I do not wish to idealize the Eastern patristic tradition, but
simply to recognize it as the base layer of all subsequent Christian exegesis and moral reflection. The major doctors of the West

from Jerome to Gregory the Great followed after and gratefully received the major orthodox formularies of the East. Remember that all of the ecumenical councils occurred east of Athens. Later writers looked east to reform the West. So it happened repeatedly with the Renaissance and Anglican forms of patristic renewal. It continues to happen today.

If Soviet scholars are astonished by this turn of events and by this interpretation of a revised Protestant problematic in religious studies, so am I. Twenty years ago if anyone had thought to asked me if American Protestants would soon be avidly reading Athanasius and John Chrysostom, I would have been puzzled by the question and thought it archaic. That was my entrenched modern chauvinism at work.

What Christians are discovering about these ancient Eastern church writers is that they have a well-formed and exquisitely nuanced hermeneutic. They speak clearly, they are well grounded textually in the biblical tradition and they are philosophically sophisticated. They are prepared to enter into a dialog with culture, and to take responsibility for cultural formation and nation-building. And they take us much more substantively into ecumenical dialogue than current dickerings of ecumenical bureaucrats.

No one can doubt that there is a great need for a renewed form of dialogue between East and West on fundamental issues of faith and practice. Now we have substantial new common ground for defining and discussing these issues. Paleo-ecumenism has become our common future.

Whether the Absence of the Protestant Experience in Soviet Society Sets an Absolute Limit to Dialog

There are only two great multicultural empires that encompass many nations and embrace within themselves myriad pluralistic cultural identities: the US and USSR. No other society is as important for us to try to understand than the Soviets, in the interest of understanding ourselves. China is more populous, but less heterogeneous. I am astonished by the tremendous variety of cultures accommodated into the Soviet megasociety. We often think of America as pluralistic, but to see authentic pluralism one must look to the Soviet Union. It is like watching a dozen rambunctious Canadas, or cuddling a hundred Yugoslavias.

I am not risking any prognostic political judgment about the future of Soviet pluralism. It is a vital and dynamic scene. Whether it can survive as a single empire or national entity, or whether it will find its way into some sort of federal system or break into smaller regional units, I cannot say. Christian historical awareness takes heart that there are many alternative forms of political organization available to the human community, not just one concept of a just social order.

Yet within all this vast Soviet pluralism, the dramatically missing element is vital, socially rooted Protestant experience of community. This is not a disapproving or berating judgment. I am not saying Soviets should have had the Protestant experience or that they should feel guilty because they have not had it. But its almost total absence makes the dialog more complicated and formidable.

As I was venturing this observation, Soviets students wanted to know more about what I meant by the Protestant experience. I define the Protestant experience as the actual life of the communities that followed the forms of biblical exegesis that stretch from Luther and Calvin through Wesley and Edwards to Martin Luther King and Billy Graham. These names are known in Soviet society, but the concrete worshiping communities they helped bring into being are not well understood. The Protestant life, with few exceptions, has not been lived out as a corporate experience in Soviet society.

I say "few exceptions" because there is indeed a hardy, modest Protestant presence in the Soviet Union, but it is extremely small relative to the whole culture. It is like asking what effect Buddhism has on contemporary American culture. It is not without effect, but there is little historical or social memory for it to build upon, unlike the West where we have had four and a half centuries of lively Protestant critique of false forms of religiosity, and sustained efforts to reshape the social order. Even the marginalized Baptist and Pentecostal expressions of Protestantism in the Soviet Union are heavily saturated with Soviet assumptions. Though no less Protestant for being in the Soviet Union, their tiny numbers relative to the whole population make them easy to ignore in the massive Soviet scheme of things. Among members of different religions in the Rostow Diocese/Province in 1972, 86% were Russian Orthodox, 5.7% were Orthodox Old Believers, and only 4.6% were a combination of Baptists, Adventists and Pentecostals.

It is not as though the Soviets were wholly without the Protestant experience, but it has come to them more as a conceptuality rather than a lengthy, unfolding historical and social process. Just as I have not had the experience of Russian Orthodoxy or atheism, except on a bookish level, they have not lived out of the Protestant ethos. They have not passionately sung "O Sacred Head Now Wounded." They have not heard a hundred sermons on the Prodigal Son. They have not marched for civil rights through the streets of a segregated city. They have not experienced their personal lives' being reborn by personal meeting with the risen Lord.

This does not mean that they cannot come as equal and respected partners into the paleo-ecumenical dialog that beckons us. For remember that we American Protestants do not have coursing so intensely in our veins the ancient archetypal memories of the Eastern church tradition which they have. We do not have the eschatological view of the mystery of the sacrament that they from birth have seen reflected in the eyes of ikons. We do not have a monastic tradition such as that which has accompanied Russian Christianity for a thousand years. We do not as often meet the risen Lord in the sacrament with such power as they do.

I found myself surprised to recognize that the former atheistic critique of czarist repression in many ways sounded reminiscent of the rhetoric of the Protestant critique of medieval sacramentalism. Remember that Protestantism developed a tough-minded denunciation of the extreme supernaturalism and antirationalism and false sacramentalism of scholastic medieval piety. This corresponds in unanticipated ways with the essential energy of the atheistic critique of all those accumulated piles of diffuse injustices committed by religions in general and by rotten social orders ambivalently allied with even the best of world religions. Soviet atheism can now be to some degree dispassionately observed and investigated from the point of view of functional sociology as a function of a struggling, once new communist order seeking to solidify its moral legitimacy.

What happened during the period of official Soviet atheism was an attempt to correct some of the extremities and injustices of the previous czarist period—corrections admittedly needed, but the attempted corrective became more costly and destructive than the oppressions it was correcting. Similarly, what happened during the declining period of American narcissistic hedonism

was an attempt to correct long-standing excesses of body negation; meanwhile these correctives tended to become even more
destructive than the ills they sought to cure.

What remains formally similar between atheistic critique of
religion and the Protestant critique of excessive sacramentalism
is the form of argument, the rhetoric, the tone of voice, the
depth of moral outrage. What is vastly more dissimilar between
these two critiques is far more decisive than any rhetorical similarities—the presence or absence of God in human history. So
upon closer inspection, the atheistic critique must be judged far
more unlike than like the Protestant critique.

I do not thereby mean to idealize a faltering Protestant ethos.
As classical Christian orthodoxy is recovering its identity the
world over, liberal American Protestantism remains entangled in
a long-term addiction to the ideological fats and sugars of modernity. To the extent that trendy ecumenism and old-line Protestant denominations have become fixated on venturing into
current public policy posturing and advising, they have succeeded
in being almost consistently wrong, hence counterproductive,
and easily dismissible. I do not look with despair on my own
liberal United Methodist denomination, as comic as its self-made
public policy dilemmas may be. Rather, I see it in a period of
lengthening twilight malaise which evokes more sadness than
contempt. Intercessory prayer seems more in order than thanks-
giving, but it is far too early for last rites. The old foundering
ship still freights many men and women with enormous gifts. It
still puzzles me that those gifts do not more often engender
leaders with the courage to challenge culture with the wisdom
of Christian Scripture and tradition.

A huge communication gap remains between postmodern
American Protestants and postatheistic Soviets. We have not had

their experience of Marxist repression, and they have not had our experience of narcissistic individualism. They have not suffered as much from the pride of arrogance and abundance as we have. They have a drug abuse crisis, but not in the vast proportion we have. Thank God for the ways in which we both have been spared.

Amid this situation, Americans need to be empathic and patient, trying our best to understand what has happened in Soviet society during the last seven decades, and not to judge or stereotype too harshly. To overcome the communication gap will require candid speaking, clear self-disclosure, and intensely accurate listening.

The Perennial Limits and Possibilities of Finite Freedom

This present circumstance in both societies mirrors the perennial paradox of finite freedom: our frail human finitude is strangely capable of soaring self-transcendence; meanwhile genuine freedom remains finitely grounded and embedded in specific, intractable historical necessities.

This particular moment of cultural struggle, whether viewed from the East or West, is more richly textured when beheld as a timely expression of the enduring human condition. A basic Christian anthropology stands ready to illuminate each intricate layer of the Soviet and American experience of sin and grace. Briefly, this anthropology holds that all of us have a body subject to empirical measuring in time and space, and at the same time, some capacity for self-transcendence, imagination, guilt, reason and memory, all of which are beyond measuring. They strain all empirical accounts. From the texts of Paul, John, and the synoptic Gospels, Christians have for centuries spoken in a code language of soul and body—of *psyche*, soul, *anima*, as that which animates body, that which makes alive this capacity for self-transcendence, and of body *(soma)* as that which houses personal life in time and space. Spirit *(ruach, pneuma)* is the dynamic interfacing of body and spirit, of finitude and freedom, of necessity and imagination. Soul and spirit are less amenable to empirical measurement than are the objects of the physical sciences, although their social and personal consequences are to some extent observable and measurable (Lactantius, *On the Workmanship of God, or the Formation of Man*, 16-20).

Soviet and American societies are wrestling with the abiding struggles of body and soul, with their perennial temptations to sensuality and pride. All of us are tempted in our finitude to become mired in sensuality, and tempted in our freedom to become inflated with pride. Human existence is a tension between the weighty drag of finiteness and the transcending reach of freedom that constitutes finite freedom (Nemesius, *On the Nature of Man)*. Both Soviet and American societies are looking for a wise equilibrium of finitude and freedom, a balance of tradition and renewal, of continuity and change, of rootedness and possibility. The task is to move toward the postmodern future, but not at panic pace.

Postmodern Christians welcome and value dialog with post-atheistic Soviets in the search for accurate description of the human condition, and in the fitting analysis of our present moral dilemmas. We are being invited to walk together into this emerging future whose outcome no one can yet see, with a basic trust that much more is at work in our historical circumstances than mundane *hubris* and *eros*. On this premise, I specifically requested their earnest prayers for me, my community of prayer, my society, and promised that I would pray for them, their university and the peace and justice of their society.

God's own Spirit is seeking to guide us toward a more complete fulfillment of our human destiny than has seemed possible under the constraints of modernity. We are not alone in this vast historical experiment. Christians believe that God participates with us in our common human sufferings.

When scoffers wonder why Christianity has been around so long yet had so little effect in changing human nature, I quietly muse that the more astonishing fact is that Christianity is around at all after all these glorious and wretched centuries in which fallen human nature has been playing itself out. That faith in the triune God has survived when so much else has failed and disappeared can only be explained by an appeal to divine providence.

PART TWO

The Critique
of Criticism

On Scientific Inquiry into Religion

*T*he conspicuous change of name of an area of humanities studies— from the Department of Atheism to the Department of the Scientific and Historical Study of Religion and Freethinking—beckons reflection and comment. This act prompts sober reflection on rightly naming and classifying what we are doing in the university when we study the artifacts and texts of religious traditions.

In this case the faculty made a symbolic decision that reaches far beyond the confines of Moscow State University. The name change suggests not only a reversal of direction of local academic policy, but a fundamental reversal of state ideology.

At one stroke and with some risk, this department of study has chosen to disavow ideological pandering, and to enter freely into that inquiry which we in the West have become accustomed to calling the scientific study of religion. Since this includes Protestant Christianity, Protestants now ironically have some indirect stake in how religion is taught in the Soviet Union. We hope it will be taught fairly, accurately, and without prejudice either in its favor or against it.

Every act of naming is itself an act of self-identification, of identity formation, of self-clarification. This decisive act of identification represents a fundamental curricular redefinition in the Humanities Division of this university. It signals that religion is now being studied in the Soviet Union not as an instrument of political policy but as a subject intrinsically worthy of unprejudiced inquiry. Once the spoiled surrogate of state ideology, this inquiry is now answering the call to reshape its methods and identity amid the intellectual challenges of the university.

It would be a mistake to imagine that a mere change of name washes away all the sins of a servile, bloody atheistic past or completely transmutes all former understandings of this faculty's discipline. But a conspicuous, symbolic first step has been taken.

It is useful to explore what sorts of scientific inquiry are fitting in the postmodern setting, especially as they pertain to the Soviet-American dialogue on religion. What follows will examine the nature of scientific inquiry into religion, prevailing methods in the study of religion, the postmodern critique of criticism, and points of contact in the Soviet-American dialogue on method.

On Proximate Empathic Objectivity
If fairness, truth seeking, and meticulous care in scholarship are

values, then the scientific inquiry into religion can never again pretend to be entirely value-free. Scientific inquiry seeks to provide a fair-minded analysis of religious communities and their forms of religious consciousness. The inquiry we share is not independent of moral values but saturated with the values of fairness in truth seeking.

Thus the scientific tradition of the study of religion does not imply an absence of value, but an active embracing of well-defined scientific values as moral premises of any effective and honest inquiry. Among these values are fairness, honesty, searching historical investigation, respect for human dignity, cross-cultural awareness, a balanced assessment of evidence, and prudence in the application of knowledge. These are moral values that guide any thoughtful inquiry. Corresponding moral disvalues that would offend against scientific inquiry are unfairness, dishonesty, biased historical investigation, disrespect for human dignity, mono-cultural awareness, a prejudiced assessment of evidence, and imprudent applications.

Good science does not entail an absolutely value-free assessment of religious communities, since honest observation and candor are moral values. Nor does good science mean investigating without any presuppositions, since existence, consciousness, and community are presuppositions of thinking. Rather the study of religion expressly demands an empathic entry into the special texts of the histories and traditions and social consequences of religious life. These texts attest divine revelation. One does not rightly study the texts of the religious tradition by ignoring or circumventing its claims of revelation, but by taking those claims seriously so as to be prepared to make responsible decisions about their alleged truthfulness.

The desired objectivity is proximate because the researcher is finite and never has all the information needed to make a completely objective assessment unencumbered by interest-laden cultural assumptions. Proximate objectivity is achieved not by discounting the object of inquiry, but by entering empathically into an unbiased examination of the object of religious inquiry. It is achieved by listening to the worshiping community's distinctive speech about itself, by scrutinizing carefully its artifacts, cultus, and dogma. The search for a scientific approach to religion does not imply a withdrawn, depersonalized, noncommittal, equivocal objectivism, but a personally engaged respect for the object of inquiry. Meanwhile, the scientific study of religion is always vulnerable to becoming prostituted by ideological presuppositions. A pretended objectivity may silently promote bias. This bias is common in American university studies in religion.

The Search for Accurate Description

What follows is best viewed not as prescriptive or normative advice from a foreigner—for I have earned no right to offer advice. Rather I offer only a straightforward description of what I see happening in American studies of religion, with a preliminary attempt to compare it with corresponding Soviet studies.

At one level the proper objects of religious inquiry are the modes of religious awareness and the communities that have emerged out of them. There is, however, another level lying silently underneath this. It has to do with accounting for the unmanipulable divine reality whom the community understands to be calling forth its life. The study of a religious community as such sometimes attempts to proceed without approaching intentionally or even closely the very divine Subject who is alleged to be the ground of that religious community and is the constant concern of its texts and prayers. When the study of religious communities occurs without any inquiry whatever into the divine ground of the religious community, an anomaly emerges. It is as if one were to attempt to study cases of law without the assumption that there is anything called "law," or to study the cases of medical diagnosis while disavowing that there is anything called "health." Viewed from within the premises of the worshiping community, it is anomalous to inquire into a redeemed community without a Redeemer, a revelation without a Revealer, a called-out community lacking any One who calls, an earnest intercession without an Listener.

The scientific study of religious communities and consciousness may or may not penetrate to the ground of inquiry as perceived by those communities. When it does, however, and when the study of religion includes rather than excludes exegesis, theology and the history of dogma, it has greater realism and heightened scientific plausibility. The grounding reality for Christians is the revelation of the triune God, the Father personally revealed in Christ crucified through the Holy Spirit.

Such an inquiry must be submitted to a different kind of critical reasoning from that which emerges merely out of human imagination and observation. Rather it understands itself to have emerged out of the actual, this-worldly, incarnational history of God's own self-disclosure. For this inquiry a narrative form of truth-telling is required. Inquiry into the language and artifacts of religion becomes more like the study of poetry or dance than laboratory experiment or mathematics, more like the analysis of truth claims of a text than simple historical data gathering. Beyond poetry, history or hermeneutics as such, this inquiry requires its own methods of truth seeking, fitting to divine self-disclosure.

A deeper objectivity is not achieved by discounting the object of religious worship or the modes of religious consciousness. It only becomes an objective inquiry by taking most seriously its object, which in this case is the incomparable, self-revealing divine Subject. Thus the paradox emerges that the greatest objectivity requires the greatest empathic personal engagement (Wilhelm Dilthey stated it concisely: historical objectivity requires an engaged entry into subjectivity). Only when I have shared most profoundly in the modes of consciousness of another do I have the right to speak of objectivity or objectively of the other. Only following an intensely empathic engagement can one begin to speak honestly of or for the other. So this paradox pervades religious inquiry: the more fully I enter into the object of inquiry with its special Subject of discourse, the more objective I can be.

The Soviets are poised to make a significant methodological contribution just at this point. They seem to more willing than American religionists to deal candidly with dogmatic formulas and traditional exegesis as legitimate concerns of inquiry into religion. Their tradition seems oddly less afraid of that territory than does American religious studies in universities, which is already committed to an ideology of a sloping playing field. On that field, those who take seriously the truth claims of classical texts are already assumed to be on the defensive lower side, while advocates of the values of Enlightenment skepticism are assumed to have the higher moral ground. These playing fields ironically are located in places with names like Notre Dame, Holy Cross, Providence and Wesleyan University, as well as Harvard, Duke and Syracuse—universities spawned by Christians.

Prevailing Western Methods of the Study of Religion
It is useful to focus directly upon methods of study of religion widely regarded as authoritative in the current American situa-

tion of religious studies, and then upon a postmodern critique of those methods. It is not necessary here to offer detailed descriptions, but only to lay out a broad map of the methodological territory, assuming all questions are open to further pursuit.

In entering this arena, I do not mean to convey that my own personal or vocational focus is directly centered upon these methods, or that these are adequate. I only wish to set forth prevailing methods by which the scientific and historical inquiry into theological and religious studies typically proceeds in the American setting. An awareness of these methods, and a proper critical response to this era of criticism, is necessary if we are to enter fully into the postmodern era. So I simply list prevailing methods without extensive comment.

There remains great interest in American religious studies in the literary critical, form critical and historical critical study of texts of Scripture and tradition. These methods are taken for granted in the American study of religion.

Literary criticism focuses upon the analysis of literary forms appearing in any given text. Form criticism seeks to provide an analysis of the oral tradition leading to the text. It attempts to grasp the structure or form by which an oral tradition has been primitively passed into a written tradition. Historical criticism of all sorts seeks to place the text in its context. Audience criticism is an attempt to show to what audience a particular text is addressed. Canon criticism asks how a body of sacred texts has come to be received as holy writ.

American religious studies tend to be rather pragmatic. Americans are normally drawn to looking at the practical results of an idea or conceptuality. Hence a prevailing approach to inquiry into religion is what might be called the pragmatic critique, which asks not about the truth question but about its practical, social

or personal result. The pragmatic method sets aside the question
of whether the truth can actually be known, and asks instead
how something functions, works, or has consequence. "Praxis"
criticism seeks to ask how ideas enter into practice and unfold in
actions. There is a growing interest in the practice of the religious life as a premise of understanding religious confession and
liturgy. One does not merely approach religion conceptually, but
must share inwardly in its community life, from within the
frame of reference of its own historical and liturgical assumptions and corporate life and cycle of seasonal celebrations. One
cannot study Zen without meditating or Judaism without study
of the rabbinic texts and seasonal rites.

The theology of culture in the tradition of Paul Tillich asks
how any expression of human culture points to an ultimate concern. One can inquire as to what ultimate concern is being inadvertently expressed in any secular activity. Many find this
method useful in analyzing the implicit religious substructures of
ostensibly secular processes. Any secular cultural expression—
such as those of art, architecture, philosophy, and psychology—
expresses ultimate concerns which may be subjected to this kind
of analysis.

Sociology of knowledge in the tradition from Karl Marx to
Max Weber and Karl Mannheim and Alfred Schutz to Peter
Berger and Thomas Luckmann seeks to understand expressions
of ideology in relation to their social location. One asks how the
knowing of something is informed by its class status and social
history.

Psychological approaches, especially psychoanalysis and behavioral psychology, continue to have a considerable effect on the
study of religion. Psychoanalysis seeks to distinguish the super-
ego, ego and libidinal contents of consciousness. Behavioral psy-

chology seeks to understand the stimulus-response patterns of learning, and to reengineer them for greater personal and social effectiveness.

Hermeneutical criticism seeks to ask how questions are being put to the text, and how the text then transforms one's questions about it. This is emerging as a unifying discipline, bringing together otherwise conflicting modes of philosophical, psychological, biographical, and historical inquiry.

Various forms of rational and philosophical criticism ask how knowing is possible, and whether that which exists may be reliably knowable. The phenomenological critique brackets out all metaphysical presuppositions and simply seeks to describe the phenomenon at hand. Linguistic analysis and logical positivism ask how a particular language game functions, or what is the descriptive status of a sentence seeking to express something meaningfully or truthfully.

By deconstructionism, we mean the dogged application of a hermeneutic of suspicion to any given text, where one finds oneself always over against the text, always asking the skeptical question about the text, asking what self-deception or bad faith might be unconsciously motivating a particular conceptuality.

Feminist criticism asks how women have been systematically barred from ideological and cultural formation, for patriarchal language models have prevailed, and how the presence of consciousness-raised women may affect the future of all other inquiries.

Aesthetic analysis asks about the style, fittingness, proportionality, symmetry, and beauty of an expression of religious worship, community, feeling or rhetoric.

The preceding account is a brisk summary, and hardly an attempt at comprehensiveness. All these methods impinge on the study of religion. Though all the above approaches have mostly unnoticed antecedents in the premodern period, all have become greatly refined and sociologically professionalized within the ethos of deteriorating modernity. Most have their own professional societies, journals, scholarly affiliations, "ol' boy" networks and insider trading.

The above methods are in some cases in a state of flux, and in other cases are in a static and defensive posture. If one takes psychoanalysis as an example, its appraisal of repression and transference has antecedents in the previous religious traditions of spiritual formation, as I have shown in *Classical Pastoral Care* (especially in the volume on *Pastoral Counsel*). After exercising protracted influence in religious circles, it has in recent decades become petrified into a defensive orthodoxy and hyperprofessionalization (as I sought to show in a 1974 study on *After Therapy What?*).

These descriptive efforts point toward a more normative moral assessment: If these are the authoritative methods available, where are they vulnerable or limited? They invite a searching critique of themselves, a critique of criticism.

Toward a Postmodern Critique of Modern Criticism

*I*n postmodern consciousness we take for granted all these available methods of modern inquiry. Postmodern orthodoxy is not a simplistic, nostalgic return to premodern methods as if modernity never happened. Rather it is a rebuilding from the ashes of modernity using treasures old and new for the restructuring process.

What makes this consciousness "post" is the fact that it does not have to go once again through the pedagogies of modernity. It has paid its dues to modernity twice over, and now is searching for meanings and truths ruled out by these methods.

There is in postmodern consciousness a growing critique of criticism, a pervasive discontent with underlying aspects of these methods of approach, especially with their moral and cultural consequences. There is also an attempt to see the survivable aspects of modern theories as having already been substantively anticipated by premodern wisdoms.

Wherever criticism's premodern antecedents have been identified, they have been systematically ignored due to our prevailing and chronic modern chauvinism. The social location analysis of John Chrysostom, for example, to my knowledge has never been the subject of a college sociology lecture. The dynamics of repression and behavior modification in Gregory the Great have never been treated in Psychology 101.

Consequently, some imagine criticism to be strictly a modern phenomenon, with no premodern antecedents. This is the premise being challenged by the critique of criticism. The idea that criticism belongs only to our own period is modern chauvinism, which systematically assumes all premodern views to be intrinsically inferior.

The Limits and Pretenses of Modern Criticism

Postmodern consciousness is unwilling to accept these modern methods uncritically. Part of the captivating game of postmodern consciousness is to puncture the myth of modern superiority, the pretense of modern chauvinism that assumes the intrinsic inferiority of all past wisdoms.

Before launching into this heavy subsection, I warn the reader that it is dense and demanding, because it assumes some awareness of the ways that modern criticism has been used and abused. With that caveat in mind, what follows are in summary form harbingers of the postmodern critique of modern criticism:

1. The postmodern orthodox critique of the *theology of culture* proceeds by asking how the revealed God transcends our ultimate concerns, and is not merely present in them. Theology of culture analysis does not sufficiently understand God as jealous of other cultural gods, and angry against the sin that flows from idolatry. An idolatrous view of an ultimate concern cannot express the proper final ground of ultimate concern. In this way a traditional, textual and exegetical critique is applied to the modern study of the theology of culture.

2. The critique of *hermeneutical criticism* asks how the interpreting process works in the case of a document alleged to be divine address. It does not hesitate to point out that the methods of modern hermeneutical analysis are largely parasitic upon the heritage of rabbinic and classic Christian exegesis of holy writ.

3. The critique of *literary critical, form critical and historical critical* study of texts of scripture and tradition asks how the economic interests, social history and value assumptions of the critic impinge upon the historical analysis. It leverages the sociology of knowledge as a basis of critique of literary, historical and aesthetic criticism. The role of historical science must be reassessed precisely amid the collapse of historical science. Postmodern historical research is as interested in the historical methods of Herodotus, Thucydides, Tacitus, Josephus, Eusebius and Theodoret of Cyprus as in modern ideologically shaped (Marxist, psychoanalytic, or deconstructionist) forms of historical criticism.

4. The critique of *audience criticism* asks how contemporary audiences have come to tyrannize over the primitive question-framing of the original audiences to which the text was once addressed. It assumes the questions of the original audiences are as legitimate and important as the questions of contemporary audiences.

5. The critique of *canon criticism* asks not merely how a text came to be viewed as holy writ, but whether it is indeed holy writ, a postmodern extension beyond the usual range of canon criticism. Thus hermeneutical criticism is employed as leverage for a critique of canon criticism.

6. The critique of *pragmatic criticism* leverages the deconstructionist critique to ask how bad faith is present in the quest for practical results and consequences, ignoring all else. It employs the psychoanalytic critique to ask how unconscious assumptions frame the very inquiries that appear to focus only upon function. It asks how the interest and social history and value system of the investigators shape the assessment of the results, thereby utilizing sociology of knowledge as the basis for a critique of *praxis*.

Don't drop out quite yet. The fun is only beginning. Think of this as a raucous roller-coaster with a few more hills and valleys ahead.

7. The critique of *sociology of knowledge* asks how knowledge elites doing the criticism have persistent, and often silent, private and class interests that shape the outcomes of the critique. Postmodern consciousness does not blush or hesitate in boldly using sociology of knowledge as a tool to investigate and disarm the sociologists of knowledge.

8. The critique of *psychoanalytic criticism* asks how effective psychoanalytic therapy is over against spontaneous remission rates, thereby applying a pragmatic critique to psychoanalysis. The critique of behaviorist criticism asks about the loss of spirit and self-transcending capacities in human existence that follow from the reduction of freedom to social and psychological necessities. Thus postmodern criticism freely makes use of the methods of classical anthropological analysis to critique behaviorism.

9. The critique of *rational philosophical criticism* asks how the in-

terest, social history and value system of the philosophical critic impinges upon the philosophical, phenomenological or logical analysis. It uses psychoanalysis and the sociology of knowledge, and even more profoundly the Jewish and Christian understanding of sin, as the basis for a critique of reason.

10. The critique of *logical and linguistic criticism* presses for the truth question underlying the language game of each sentence or the logical status of a particular utterance. It asks how the interest and social history and value system of the logical analyst impinges upon the analysis. It does not hesitate to point out that the methods of modern linguistic analysis were anticipated by rabbinic and classical Christian exegesis. Long before A. J. Ayer and L. Wittgenstein, the rabbis of the Mishnaic period and the Christian exegetes of the patristic period were patiently taking apart sentences, especially of holy writ and tradition, looking for their meaning and function, elaborating on their unrecognized or neglected nuances.

11. The critique of *deconstructionist criticism* asks how the interest and social history and value system assumed in the deconstruction impinge upon the analysis. It uses moral criticism as a basis of critique of deconstructionism.

12. The postfeminist critique of *feminist criticism* asks how physiological sexual differentiation research affects unisex theories and hyperegalitarian logic, and how women have been significant shapers of traditional cultures.

13. The critique of *aesthetic criticism* asks how the aesthete deals with morality and suffering, thereby leveraging a moral and spiritual critique as the basis for a critique of aesthetics, placing the question of beauty in juxtaposition to the question of the truth of the revealed word.

And so it goes. Postmodern consciousness does not hesitate to enter the methodological fray, play devil's advocate, cause general trouble, and be ready when necessary to announce: "The emperor has no clothes." Modernity, which thought itself so handsomely furnished with fancy attire, ostentatious theories, and elaborate methods of research, is feeling ever more exposed and unmasked.

In all these ways, and more, the fashionable modes of criticism are being found vulnerable to a candid postmodern critique of modern forms of criticism. This opens the way for a deepened inquiry into the truth claims of classical Jewish and Christian texts. The postmodern ethos is in many ways a postcritical situation.

Detractors may caricature postmodern paleoorthodox consciousness as precritical. I say postcritical. In my own case, it is far too late to be precritical if one has already spent most of one's life pursuing modern critical inquiries, "chasing rabbits" of critical theories based on the premises of modern chauvinism (that newer is always better, older worse). That can no longer be precritical which follows after assimilating two centuries of modern naturalistic and idealistic criticism. If merely to use sources that emerged before a modern period called "the age of criticism" is to be precritical then in that sense I delight in being precritical, but note how damning that premise is to the integrity of modern criticism, if it supposes that one is able only to use sources of one's own historical period.

Points of Contact in the Soviet-American Dialog on Method

Amid this postcritical situation, a startling opportunity is being offered religious studies to enter the university dialog with new energy. This applies to studies in religion in Soviet as well as American settings.

It is useful to ask to what degree Russian and Soviet sources and methods are being taken into account in the American study of religion. Marx and Lenin are being studied as historical figures in political science circles, but less as viable constructive theorists, and seldom directly in religious studies. But a Marxian analysis of class struggle remains a pivotal tool for analysis among liberation theologians, deconstructionists, historical revisionists, existentialists and advocates of sociology of knowledge. The form of Marxism that survives in American universities is largely a sentimental dream of aging radicals. These voices are occasionally heard but in a defensive tone replete with disclaimers.

Lenin is not often read but has had a sobering effect upon the study of religion as the main systems-designer of a social engineering strategy that has despite its rhetoric become repressive on a preposterously immense scale. Lenin's work on the social basis of religion in capitalism is generally accorded a key role in the history of the study of atheism, along with his criticism of the bourgeois-clerical falsification of scientific atheism.

It is fitting in this context to ask how Russian and Soviet sources have influenced or affected these modes of inquiry. Ironically, the tradition of Marxist economics is probably more alive in American university and church circles than in Soviet circles. Castro and Ortega would receive a warmer reception in Stanford than Moscow. Mao and Che are more revered at 475 Riverside Drive than in Tiananmen Square or the hills of El Salvador. Moscow has had to suffer much more concretely and directly from Marxist follies. Our knowledge elites still have the blessed privilege of treating Marxist notions as untested theory—this cannot be said of Soviet academics.

Non-Marxist Russian Contributions

If we are speaking of non-Marxist Russian and Soviet sources, the story is different. They continue to have considerable impact on American methods and viewpoints in the study of religion. Among them certain figures remain highly respected for insights into religious communities and dynamics.

Dostoyevsky remains the unexcelled portrayer of the intriguing characters of Russian consciousness, and in some ways one of the earliest heralds of postmodern consciousness. He intuitively sensed the eventual demise of modernity long before it had begun to decline. Solzhenitzyn has envisioned the spiritual promise of the Russian tradition better than anyone since Soloviev. Yevtushenko is often read as a poet of transition, voicing the pathos and aspiration of the Soviet people for a more person-oriented social system. Chekhov is still seen frequently on American stages as the principal interpreter of the pathos of a dying prerevolutionary social order. Tolstoy expresses the purist form of that pacifist ascetic idealism that has found its way into the views of Gandhi and Martin Luther King, Jr. Pavlov remains the pivotal figure in the early history of behavioral psychology. Rachmaninoff, Tchaikovsky, and Shostakovich are preeminent musical voices in the transition of modern music from romanticism to creative dissonance.

Among older Russian theological writers, Soloviev and Berdyaev are still intently read in some circles. Paris emigres like Georges Florovsky and Alexander Schmemann, who helped bring the Russian Orthodox tradition into the ecumenical movement, are enjoying ever-widening reading audiences. There is a new edition of Florovsky now in English, and he is likely to remain the major interpreter of the Russian religious tradition. Kallistos Ware, John Meyendorff, John Breck and

Thomas Hopko are worthy English-speaking inheritors of that profound Russian tradition of spirituality. The *Philokalia* tradition is being actively studied. *The Way of the Pilgrim* remains a popular text on meditation and pilgrimage.

At Drew University, for example, we have a joint Ph.D. program with St. Vladimir's Orthodox Seminary, which brings the Russian tradition directly into our study of liturgy. Alexander Schmemann was St. Vladimir's former dean; John Meyendorff, the present dean, and its professors, Thomas Hopko and John Breck, are enlarging the Orthodox tradition in exegesis and ecumenical dialogue. These are some of the influences of Russian literature in our setting, and one expects more as glasnost proceeds.

In these chapters so far, we have defined modernity, postmodernity, Christian consciousness within postmodernity, and offered a postmodern critique of modern criticism. In reflecting on the shape of postmodern Christian consciousness, we may begin to wonder whether the fundamental structure of human nature is changing, and what may remain intact of the Christian view of human nature. So, looking ahead, we will be asking how the fundamental make-up of the human condition in time shapes the emerging dialogue. This leads us to a rudimentary reflection upon the structure of human temporal awareness, and how it correlates with classical Christian understandings.

The Human Predicament in Time

CHAPTER
SIX

Transcending Anxiety, Guilt and Boredom

What follows in this and the next chapter is an uncomplicated description of the way the human self moves within time, how awareness functions within temporal limits, and how the work of the Holy Spirit affects and changes every layer of human awareness in time.

This exercise gives us an opportunity to demonstrate how postmodern Christian consciousness is free to utilize modern forms of hermeneutic, existential and phenomenological analysis, without being taken captive to them. I will use these methods as a springboard for another more substantive concern—to listen

anew amid postmodern culture to the texts of Christian scripture and tradition. We will walk step by step through the human
predicament in time, then show how that predicament is being
altogether transformed by the Christian proclamation. Consider
these steps as a series of definitions which seek to distinguish:

a value	guilt
a center of value	intensified guilt
a god	the guilt/anxiety symmetry
idolatry	a temporal limit
death	the human predicament
God	finite freedom
time	now
possibility	experience
anxiety	boredom
past	despair
memory	

To grasp these terms rightly and in their proper sequence is to
lay hold of the fundamental make-up of the human condition in
time. We will look together at twenty-one definitions of human
selfhood in time.

The Valuing, Idolatrous Self

1. Every self exists in relation to values perceived as making life
worth living. A *value* is anything good in the created order—any
idea, relation, object or person in which one has an interest, from
which one derives significance, or in relation to which one feels
an enduring sense of obligation.

2. These values compete. One finite value often comes to exercise power or preeminence over other values. In time one is

prone to choose a *center of value* by which other values are judged.

3. When a finite value has been elevated to centrality and imagined as a final source of meaning, then one has chosen what Jews and Christians call *a god*, whereby some finite value is being treated as that than which nothing more valuable can be conceived (Irenaeus, *Against Heresies*, 5.16; Tertullian, *On Idolatry*, 1-4).

Any finite good can become a potential idolatry. To be worshiped as a god, something must be sufficiently good to be plausibly regarded as the rightful center of one's valuing. Otherwise it is not even a decent candidate for idolatry. That which has no power to tempt us to worship it is not good enough to become a credible potential idolatry. If education were not a source of enormous good, it would not tempt us to make it a god. If one's motherland, regional identity or family tradition were not exceptionally meaningful, it would not tempt us to make it a center of value. But precisely because these things are of such inestimable value to us, they tempt us toward idolatry. Were my daughter not a source of exceptional affection and delight, she would not be a potential idolatry for me, but I am tempted to adore her in a way we both know is disproportional. One has a god when a finite value is worshiped and adored and viewed as that without which one cannot receive life joyfully (Augustine, *City of God*, 19.25; *On the Profit of Believing*, 14).

4. We are constantly taking good things—relationships, sex, music, food, political aspirations, hometown, clique—and viewing them as if they were "that than which nothing greater can be conceived" (Anselm, *Proslogion*, 2). *Idolatry* is the elevation of any finite value to a pretended ultimacy (Tertullian, *On Idolatry*, 1). Idolatry treats a limited value as if it were absolute (Augustine, *Enchiridion*, 4-9). Under stress, the self is at times torn apart by competition between its various gods.

5. These creaturely values and goods deteriorate and ultimately die. They die because they are finite. *Death* is structured into their finitude. These are merely finite goods we are worshiping. They are derived from personal choices in collusion with historical determinants. All disappear (Athanasius, *Against the Heathen*, 10-27).

6. That-out-of-Which all these finite values come, and That-into-Which all finite values disappear and perish, is what Jews and Christians call God (Yahweh in Hebrew, Theos in Greek, Deus in Latin, Bog in Russian, Gott in the Teutonic languages, and in English, God). The sparest definition I know of *God* is *That-out-of-Which and That-into-Which*—the incomparable One out of which come and into which go all things. Only this One is that than which nothing greater can be conceived (Anselm, *Proslogion*). This One is not a finite value but the giver of all finite values, who remains after all finite values are spent (John of Damascus, *Orthodox Faith*, 1.9; Calvin, *Institutes*, 3.20). Only this One is worthy of worship (H. R. Niebuhr, *Radical Monotheism and Western Culture*).

The Future

7. The human self exists in time. *Time* is the interval between any two events, during which something exists, happens or acts. The broadest definition of time is that interval between creation and the hypothesized end of time (Origen, *Against Celsus*, 6.42). The historical self experiences time in a highly personal sense as that interval between one's own individual birth and death.

Being cast in time, the self exists in relation to the future. One has no choice as a temporal being other than to live in relation to one's specific and personal future. That future one does not govern or manage but meets and deals with moment by moment (Augustine, *City of God*, 14.27).

The self does not merely *have* time, it *is* a relation to time. The self is constituted as a self in relation to its own particular time, and the personal faces and voices that have filled that time from childhood forward (Augustine, *Confessions*, 1-3).

8. The self exists constantly in relation to *possibility*. That which is possible can be, or is thought capable of coming to be. Possibility is a category of the future. No possibility dwells in the past, only in the future. Imagination reaches out for possibility (John of Damascus, *Orthodox Faith*, 2.25-28).

Anxiety

9. When I interpret some particular possibility as a threat to some value I consider necessary for my existence, I experience *anxiety*. Anxiety is that relation to the future in which through imagination I experience possibility as a threat to my being (John Chrysostom, *Homilies on St. John*, 75; Augustine, *Letters*, 186, FC 30).

Anxiety becomes neurotically intensified to the degree that I have idolized finite values that properly should have been regarded as limited (John Climacus, *Ladder of Divine Ascent*, 4.118). The more I worship finite gods, the more I make myself vulnerable to intensified anxiety (Ps 139:23-24; Augustine, *Exposition on Psalm 139*).

When I view a particular possibility as threatening, it imperils some value important to me. That is what I mean by threat. But suppose this threat is directed not to some modest finite value I love, but to the very center of my value system, that focal value by which all my other values are viewed as valuable (John Cassian, *First Conference of Abbot Chaeromon*, 13). Suppose my god is sex or my own physical health or the Democratic Party. If I experience one of these as under genuine threat, then I feel myself shaken to the depths. In this way, idolatry intensifies anxiety.

The dysfunctional syndrome is increased to the degree that I have taken these values and made of them gods (John Climacus, *Ladder of Divine Ascent*, 26).

The Past

10. Every self exists in relation to its *past*. I have no choice but to live with my past, for I am a relation with my past. The past is that entire interval of time which is over, gone, accomplished. A person's past is one's former life in time (Augustine, *Confessions*, 3-8).

11. The relation I have with the past is constituted experientially by the layers of *memory* that I have of my own specific personal past, for which I am responsible. Through recollection I recall my past. Through historical documentation and law and corporate memory, this memory can extend far beyond my own life to a familial and social and national and global and even paleological and cosmic history in which I concretely participate (Lactantius, *Divine Institutes*, 68ff.; Gregory Nazianzen, *Orations*, 2.28-33).

Guilt

12. Since human existence is a choosing existence, it is necessarily a value-negating existence, and thus an existence bound up in guilt (Augustine, *Ennarations on Psalms*, 38). I realize that I in my free self-determination hold myself responsible for negating values that I regard as necessary for my existence. When I interpret the past as a negation of the very values I hold most dear and that make my life meaningful, I experience *guilt* (Tertullian, *On Penitence*). I relate myself to my past through memory in the form of guilt (Augustine, *Confessions*, 3-5).

13. Guilt becomes neurotically intensified to the degree that I

have idolatrized finite values that properly should have been regarded as limited. The more I worship finite gods, the more I
make myself vulnerable to *intensified guilt* (Ps 51; John Chrysostom, *Baptismal Instructions*).

Suppose I value my ability to communicate clearly. I feel responsible for accurate speech. Suppose I become aware that at
this moment I am not communicating very clearly. I feel a tinge
of guilt. But suppose clear communication has become an absolute value for me, a center of value that makes all my other
values valuable. Then if I utter a sentence that I know does not
make good sense, I may be stricken with neurotic guilt. For then
I have negated not merely a finite value, but a value I am responsible for idolizing (Gregory the Great, *Pastoral Care*, 3).

The Symmetry of Anxiety and Guilt

14. Guilt and anxiety are the two defining problems of the self
in relation to its personal past and future. I cannot avoid facing
the hazards of possibility and I cannot avoid the impinging memory of having at times negated, diminished or neglected those
values I regard as important for my self-fulfillment.

Thus we discover a surprising *symmetry of guilt and anxiety.* Guilt
and anxiety are dialectical opposites, performing directly parallel
and analogous converse functions in time. Each is so diametrical-
ly opposite its contrary that it functions exactly like its contrary
as a mirroring antithesis. This is why guilt and anxiety are so
similar—precisely because they are so systematically different.

This is a simple, fundamental observation much neglected in
contemporary psychotherapeutic literature: guilt is directed toward the past and anxiety toward the future, so as to constitute
the defining human problems resulting from consciousness in
time. One would expect that such a simple observation would

already be thoroughly investigated, but one looks in vain for a definitive treatment of it. Despite a vast bibliography on guilt and anxiety, their basic parallelism and dialectical relation to temporality have not been well understood (Oden, *The Structure of Awareness*, 6, 20.2-3, 22.3).

When the self symbolizes its approaching possibilities as a threat to values considered necessary for living toward its future, one experiences anxiety. Oppositely, when the self symbolizes remembered events as irresponsible negations of values considered necessary for living with its past, then one experiences guilt.

15. These temporal antitheses function within strict *temporal limits*. This is why it is impossible to be guilty toward a future possibility, or to be anxious toward a past actuality. An emotive response has a temporal limit if it is limited strictly either to time past or time future. Guilt and anxiety function under stringent temporal limits. Guilt is unable to extend itself into the future— that is not its native temporal arena. Anxiety has no home in the past. It only exists in relation to the future. It is only when guilt is grasped by analogy with anxiety that its fundamental structure as temporal is understood, and the temporal nature of the self is beheld.

16. The essential *human predicament* in relation to the future is an ever-extending yearning to control what is uncontrollable, namely, open possibility. The fundamental human predicament in relation to the past is the wish to undo that which is done, namely, the closed book of the past, anything past. We vainly wish to predict, fix, know and predetermine the future, which is by definition unknowable and undeterminable. Snared in time, we despair over wishing to form the future and reform the past. This is the absurd folly and temptation of human imagination and memory, that it seeks either to undo the done or secure the

unsecurable (Augustine, *Confessions*, 10).

The future is empty, undetermined, open possibility where nothing is yet fixed. The past is filled, fixed, immutable, closed, completely determined by its having passed through some present moment. That, in fact, is all that we mean by the past, anything that has passed through some living present moment into time past (Augustine, *Confessions*, 11).

What we call past is constantly undergoing present reinterpretation, but the salient point is that this remembering process occurs exclusively in the present, not the past. The past as such remains immutable. It is precisely the dead, fixed and immutable character of the past that places its most compelling claim upon the present, impinging upon memory as a leech (Clement of Alexandria, *Christ the Educator*, 2.2).

17. Were there no such thing as death, then all present decisions would be relatively meaningless, for then one could postpone any decision indefinitely (Lactantius, *On the Workmanship of God*, 4). Present decision can have meaning only on the premise that it is finite and has a definite terminus in time. Human decision making, hence human freedom, would be neither free nor meaningful if every decision were infinitely revisable. Death is that point at which all decisions become unrevisable (John Chrysostom, *Eutropius*).

Freedom is free and meaning is meaningful precisely under the limitations of finitude. If any past decision could be infinitely reworkable and revisitable, then there could be no such thing as value negation and guilt or risk and anxiety, or even freedom in a meaningful sense. *Finite freedom* becomes meaningful and serious only when the self exists within a finite temporal order with bodily death as its terminus, aware that it is responsible for what it deposits in its past, and ultimately to be called to judgment

(Irenaeus, *Against Heresies*, 5.8). Once something becomes past, it has passed beyond our grasp and become concretized in unrevisable time (Ambrose, *On Belief in the Resurrection*, 2.124).

The Present as Experience

18. Though strictly speaking human awareness always exists in the present, it is constantly being drawn toward the fantasizing of dreaded future possibilities and the mourning of past actualities. This is the perennial temptation of freedom in the present. That is *now* which is present in time at this fleeting moment (Augustine, *Confessions*, 11). Abraham Cowley rightly grasped that

Nothing is there to come, and nothing past,
But an eternal now does ever last.

My present is missed or misplaced because I become so preoccupied with imagination of future contingencies that I fixate constantly upon unmet and unmeetable possibilities. Then I am stuck in anxiety. My present capacity for value actualization is distorted when I become so preoccupied with the recollection of past actualities that present consciousness becomes fixated upon past value negations. Then I am stuck in guilt.

19. Meanwhile I always actually exist concretely only in the present. My relation to the present is *experience*, that which is being lived through, my actual living through an event, my personal undergoing, feeling, and observing of something as it occurs. Present experience is precisely what is happening in my relation to my present—whatever is now occurring. I am now experiencing this room, its lights and shadows, interpersonal contact with my partners in dialog, and the world of language between us. This is my present experience. When one speaks of an experience as past, or the whole of one's experience, what is

meant is the memory of something once present, whatever has actually occurred and been lived through in some lively present (Augustine, *Confessions*, 4).

Boredom

20. When I interpret my present experience as empty of meaning, when nothing of value to me is occurring, then I relate to the present in the form of boredom. *Boredom* is the state of being wearied or annoyed by the present.

I am bored if I interpret my present as empty of any value crucial to me. To be bored is to feel empty. Nothing of any perceived importance is happening when one is bored. Boredom is an anticipatory form of being dead (John Cassian, *Institutes*, 9, 10). The central aesthetic problem of the self in the present is boredom. We go to great lengths to avoid boredom.

21. When relative values become absolutized, elevated to ultimate centers of value, boredom is prone to becoming intensified. To the extent to which limited values are exalted to idolatries, the destructive capacity of boredom becomes magnified. When the present is felt to be devoid of values that have become falsely absolutized, boredom becomes pathological and compulsive, and despair of freedom a preoccupation. Idolatrous boredom exaggerates the limitations of the present, applying to the now the symbols of emptiness. My subjectively experienced boredom may then become infinitely projected toward the whole cosmos as if everything were objectively meaningless. Radical boredom falsely focuses consciousness upon the whole human and cosmic condition, as if everything were devoid of meaning (John Cassian, *Institutes*, 9, 10).

The structure of human consciousness in time gives to the human predicament its specific character. The hell of human consciousness in time may be summarized as a boring present, an anxious future, and a guilty past. These debilitating forms of awareness appear to be eternal, although they exist in time. We imagine our entire lives to be unremittingly bored, dreadfully anxious, and locked in demoralizing, neurotic guilt. This picture of the self is called *despair*. Such is the human predicament in time (Kierkegaard, *The Sickness unto Death*).

It is this predicament to which Christianity brings good news. Layer upon layer, as the self falls into sin and death and anxiety and guilt and boredom, the gospel of God reaches out to rescue the self from fallenness (Cyril of Jerusalem, *Catechetical Lectures*, 2).

Soviet and American Variations on Anxiety, Guilt and Boredom

This structural interpretation of the human predicament correlates with the cultural conditions we have been addressing in this book—postmodern Soviet and American megasocieties. The governing thesis: While the specific content of anxiety, guilt, and boredom changes from culture to culture and time to time and ideology to ideology, its basic form remains the same.

These differences deserve specific illustration: Soviets are more likely to become intensely anxious about getting on a three-year waiting list for a small apartment than Americans, who are more likely to feel all uptight about getting in a three-minute line to complain about customer service. Americans are more likely to become apprehensive about long-term planning for high tuition expenses to a drug-free college for their children than Soviet parents, who are more likely to feel uneasy about just getting potatoes and bread for the family for the next few days.

Soviets are more likely to feel guilty about burdening personal friendships with the special trials of a barter economy than

Americans, who are more likely to feel guilty about fudged tax returns or speeding in a school zone or concealed information in an insurance report. Americans are more likely to feel tinges of guilt over an unmowed lawn or a unwashed automobile than Soviet citizens, who are more likely to feel guilty about venturing into an open market exchange or political demonstration.

Soviets are more likely to be bored with an hour-long daily commute on a packed subway than Americans, who are more likely to feel bored with the slightly uneven quality of the stereo system in the comfortable car in which they make their twenty-minute commute to work. Americans are more likely to be bored with the taste of a fast-food hamburger than Soviet citizens, who are more likely to feel that such a hamburger would be the high point of a week, but bored with waiting in a block-long line for underwear.

While these differences may seem dramatic in tone, the formal structure of anxiety, guilt, and boredom in each case is extremely similar. The guilt-anxiety symmetry functions dependably in each of these cases. Now we ratchet up the question to contrast tendencies of modern as opposed to postmodern consciousness. Here are typical differences in the tonality of guilt, anxiety, and boredom in the emerging situation:

1. Older Soviet citizens of recent *mod rot* decades have been prone to be extremely *anxious* about staying within bounds of the rhetoric of communist ideology. In contrast, the emerging *postmodern* Soviet citizen has largely forgotten that anxiety, and is now more prone to be anxious about how the country is going to achieve a stable political democracy and develop a reliable system of free market exchange where goods and services are available and marketable.

2. While Soviet parents of late modernity have been prone to

feel easily *guilty* about any hint of political uniqueness or individuality, emerging postmodern Soviet parents are more likely to feel guilty about why they have not been able to provide decent consumer goods and comfortable homes and food for their growing families.

3. While the late modern Soviet worker has been prone to be easily *bored* by daily factory routines, the emerging postmodern Soviet worker is more likely to become bored with the rhetoric of atheism and revolution, and to spoof its comic side.

Here are typical differences in the tonality of guilt, anxiety, and boredom in the emerging postmodern American generation, as distinguished from the passing generation:

1. Older Americans of *mod rot* decades have been prone to be overly *anxious* about material success, safe jobs, upward mobility, active sexuality, and social security. In contrast, emerging *postmodern* American citizens are tending to become more anxious about the quality of their personal bonding and parenting, their family-building and nurturing, their personal intimacy and spiritual formation.

2. While Americans of late modernity have been prone to feel easily *guilty* about fun, unproductivity, and financial failure, emerging postmodern American parents are more likely to feel guilty about their lack of fun, their being locked into uninteresting forms of economic productivity, and why they seem unable to provide a healthy moral atmosphere for their children that will keep them relatively protected from life-threatening abuses—muggings, rape, AIDS and homosexuality.

3. The passing generation of American workers has been prone to be easily *bored* by problems of production, such as the repetitiousness of the assembly line, while the emerging American worker is more likely to become bored with limitations re-

lating to problems of consumption, such as healthful food, decent entertainment, clean air, and good music.

While these illustrations point out differences in tonality between specific experiences of anxiety, guilt and boredom, the formal structure of human consciousness in time in each case is intergenerationally similar, with the guilt-anxiety symmetry functioning steadily throughout.

Having briefly illustrated some varieties of the corrosive human predicament in time, we have next the task of specifying how the Christian message addresses it as good news, and how the Holy Spirit works to transform it layer by layer.

The Christian Answer to Boredom: Forgiveness, Trust and Responsive Love

*C*hristian spiritual formation deals constantly with precisely these fundamental problems of the basic relation of human existence in time (Gregory the Great, *Pastoral Care*, 2). Three points concisely summarize the reversal of consciousness in time that is enabled by the good news of God in Jesus Christ.

Forgiveness: The End of Guilt

Guilt toward the past is transmuted by *forgiveness* (Leo I, *Sermons*, 49). God takes upon himself the burden and weight of our guilt. God the Son is voluntarily sacrificed for us so that our guilt becomes vicariously borne by him (Clement of Alexandria, *Christ the Educator*, 1.8-10). The self is thereby offered a new freedom to embrace the past, to move through and beyond guilt into not merely self-acceptance but also reconciliation with God the Father, That Out-of-Which and Into-Which all things flow, than which nothing greater can be conceived (Tertullian, *On Penitence;* Anselm, *Proslogion).* I can move through the awareness of the irresponsible negation of my values, beyond guilt to forgiveness, whereby I receive myself anew despite my guilt (Irenaeus, *Against Heresies,* 2).

But how is it possible to come reliably to know that one is forgiven? Here one must tell a story, a history of events through which that forgiveness is made known. The decisive event is the cross (John of Damascus, *Orthodox Faith,* 4.11). Forgiveness begins with the cross understood as applying to me (Gregory Nazianzen, *Oration,* 36.1).

Revelation of Divine Pardon

In Christian understanding, we can only know God if God chooses to become personally self-revealed. Lacking revelation, there is no knowledge of God, except for the crumbs available through natural reasoning, or inference from finitude, through the so-called negative way of knowing God (Cyril of Jerusalem, *Catechetical Lectures,* 16.2, 17.1).

In interpersonal relationships we can choose either to reveal or withhold ourselves. It is a choice. I do not have to reveal myself to anyone. I can withdraw. I do at times withdraw. But I can take the risk of revealing myself. Some people reveal themselves compulsively all the time, like a diarrhea. God is not constantly self-revealed. God is revealed modestly, appropriately, and with constraints proper to God's holy love (Athanasius, *On the Incarnation of the Word*).

Christian worship is based upon an accumulation of remembered experiences. Canonical Scripture recalls these events which illuminate all prior and subsequent human experience (Irenaeus, *Against Heresies*, 4). These primordially revelatory experiences can be made the subject of scientific and historical investigation. There is no reason anyone should be blocked from investigating any aspect (social, historical, economic, philosophical, linguistic) of the recollection of these experiences (Origen, *On First Principles*, Preface). But since the empirical method observes, records, and analyzes objects and not persons, it is not possible to analyze the intended subject of the text, the revealing God, for God is not an object, like other objects of finite inquiry. God is personal subject, not object (Basil, *On the Holy Spirit*, 1.14). The personal God is unknowable except as God comes to make himself known.

The narrative of this coming is the story told in Scripture, canonically and ecumenically received by a believing community attentive to the earliest layers of its traditional interpretation (Irenaeus, *Against Heresies*, 2,3). Here we learn the story of One who comes to meet us in our guilt, anxiety, and boredom with a freeing word that enables forgiveness, trust, and responsive openness to presently unfolding experience.

The stain of sin reaches into all forms of historical suffering. No moment in time is unstained by sin. But however shaped by whatever absurdities, suffering can by grace be made meaningful and redemptive (Augustine, *On Free Will*, 3). I suffer and by my insensitivities cause others to suffer. There is no suffering that I undergo or cause that God has not already undergone and embraced with his forgiveness. This is the meaning of the incarnation and cross, Christmas and Easter. God has taken upon himself our human condition and suffered for us (Irenaeus, *Against Heresies*, 5.1; Leo I, *Letter to Flavian*).

By forgiveness suffering is transmuted. Though I cause others to suffer by excessively asserting my interest, God takes that sin upon himself in the cross. All human suffering is viewed in the light of God suffering with and for us (Cyril of Jerusalem, *Catechetical Lectures*, 13).

The premise of Christian reasoning is not that we have discovered God through our superior intellectual efforts, but that God becomes personally self-revealed in history as one who loves sinners with an incomparably holy love despite all our obstinacies (Origen, *Against Celsus*, 4.28; John of Damascus, *Orthodox Faith*, 1.7, 4.4). We actively resist knowing God, because God's good news challenges all our pretenses to self-sufficiency and imagined autonomy (Gregory the Great, *Pastoral Care*, 3). But God comes anyway to meet us in the form of a servant. God enters our human sphere, shares our context, our vulnerable frame, our suffering (Gregory Nazianzen, *Orations*, 29.19). Paul invited the Philippians in this text to have that same mind that was in Christ Jesus:

Who, being in the very nature God,
did not consider equality with God
something to be grasped,
but made himself nothing, taking the very
nature of a servant,
being made in human likeness.
And being found in appearance as a man,
he humbled himself
and became obedient to death—
even death on a cross!
Therefore God exalted him to the highest place

and gave him the name that is above every name,
that at the name of Jesus every knee should bow,
in heaven and on earth and under the earth,
and every tongue confess that Jesus Christ is Lord,
to the glory of the Father. (2:5-11 NIV)

Trust: The End of Anxiety

Christianity sees idolatrously intensified anxiety as a distortion of the human condition in relation to the future. There is no reason aside from self-chosen idolatries that we are destined to be neurotically anxious. Anxiety is groundless, when viewed from the vantage point of trust in God's trustworthiness beyond the collapse of our gods (Augustine, *Expositions on Psalms*, 139). In Christian understanding, God is calling us to go through this anxiety to receive possibility anew as our own, and thereby to accept ourselves as free with commensurable risks (Job 13:15; Athanasius, *On the Incarnation of the Word*).

The confidence by which one embraces one's personal future is *trust*—Greek: *pistis*, faith, primordial trust. Only by learning to trust the One who gives life is one freed to engage once again in the risk-laden movement toward possibility (John of Damascus, *Orthodox Faith*, 3.9).

Freedom's awareness of its own risks and vulnerabilities is compared by Kierkegaard to picturing oneself as standing on the edge of a cliff. When I draw near the edge of the abyss, so as to recognize that I am experiencing a hazard and thus become aware of the risk side of my freedom, I tend to turn away in anxiety. When I turn away, I hear my self pronouncing myself guilty for turning away from possibility (Kierkegaard, *The Concept of Anxiety*). Christian faith invites us not to turn away from beholding the risks of freedom but rather to embrace these risks when necessary, even unto death, trusting the giver of freedom (John Chrysostom, *Homilies on Hebrews*, 12).

How does one come to learn to trust in the unknown future? Here one must recollect a history of events through which God's own trustworthiness is made known beyond the death of all finite values. The trust in God seen in the dying, risen Lord is the fundamental pattern of trust in each momentary situation where trust is required (Cyril of Jerusalem, *Catechetical Lectures*, 13,14; Augustine, *Enchiridion*). The Word of God comes to us in the form of a history. Knowing God is a narrative form of knowing. It is not a speculative, undynamic or depersonalized form of knowing, but a personal knowing of a person revealed. Thus faith is received through the telling of a personal history (Origen, *Against Celsus*, 1.11).

So Jews and Christians recall narrative histories of Joseph being put into the pit and Moses leading the people of Israel across the Red Sea, and Abraham taking Isaac to the mountain to be sacrificed, and Jesus being tempted and dying on a cross. We recite these histories in order to understand how we have been met by this personal One, who called himself simply "I am who I am." We are finally met by this One in the incarnate Lord (Athanasius, *On the Incarnation of the Word*).

But if Christ has come, why do we persist in feeling pointlessly guilty, anxious and bored, supposing that all these feelings are finally based merely upon an absurd idolatry? Christians understand this recalcitrance as the vain resistance we continue to have to God's own gracious coming and speaking (John Chrysostom, *Baptismal Instructions*). Sin is precisely our turning our back on the actually revealed goodness of God. It is the choice to remain anxious and guilty even when the ground of anxiety and guilt has in fact already been undercut by the eventful, forgiving love of God (Athanasius, *Resurrection Letters*, 5).

Must one experience the death of one's gods in order to move toward faith? Is this trust possible only in the light of this story of meeting with this particular one, Jesus Christ? Why could not it occur without this history? Christians do not put limits on the power of the Holy Spirit by pretending that God cannot work except in those specific ways that we confirm or find familiar. The Spirit, being omnipresent in human history, has other ways of working than through our proclamation, baptism, and justifying faith (Clement of Alexandria, *Stromata*, 1.21; *Westminster Confession*, 10). But for Christian worshipers, the place where that unconditional love has been revealed most clearly is in the cross.

The claim of classical Christian teaching is not that there can be no activity of God apart from our memory of the cross, but that the cross reveals, in an unexcelled way, the heart of God toward lost and sinful humanity (John Chrysostom, *Homilies on St. John*, 8.1).

I am not woodenly saying that one must experience the death of one's gods before becoming a person of faith. But most of us do have experiences of this sort. We all feel loss, and mourn the negation of our absolutized values. I do not commend death or claim that it is a wonderful thing. I wish that many of my finite values might last a very long time. It is a tempting but vain thought to think that my daughter will never die. But of course, she will die as I will die. The certainty of death is given in and with life, as an intrinsic aspect of the gift of finite existence. If we did not have death we would not be finite. Admittedly death feels like a sinister and awesome reality, especially from the point of view of our gods. But life in Christ is not life lived in fear, even of death (1 John 4:18).

I had coronary surgery on July 17, 1989. They cut me down

the middle, opened me up, went into the coronary arteries, took out those plugged up, and inserted an unobstructed artery taken from my leg, devising a three-way bypass of clogged-up arteries. I almost died. I am incredibly fortunate and blessed simply to be here.

I learned something wonderful from that. I would not have learned it had I not been in that situation of extreme limitation. What I learned is simple: I am not afraid to die. I did not know that before this experience. I did not have anything that I could describe as an out-of-body experience, or a beyond-death experience or any unusual or paranormal sort of premonition or precognitive experience. My awareness of death was completely conscious and based upon simple observation. I woke up after the surgery so weak I could hardly raise my finger. I was hooked up to biofeedback equipment that signaled when I was exerting too much energy. I could set off the buzzer by simply raising my hand. But the pivotal lesson hinged on a New Testament text: that God's "grace is sufficient for you, for [God's] strength is made perfect through our weakness" (2 Cor 12:9). I learned that through this experience.

Responsive Love: The End of Boredom

Boredom is overcome by reentering present experience on the premise that it is abundantly full of actualizable values, even amid limitations. One who glimpses anew the present moment as overflowing gift of divine grace cannot remain bored (Augustine, *Confessions*, 4, 10). In every moment, however limiting, God is offering special, unrepeatable gifts for human self-actualization (Augustine, *Faith and Works*, 16; *Homilies on John*, Tractate 6).

God is thus self-revealed as partner, advocate and comforter within each moment of present history. Every present moment is objectively laden with a profusion of values to be actualized, even when one may subjectively ignore or disdain them. We cannot live otherwise than amid the fullness of God in the present, even when we refuse to recognize or respond to that fullness. This now is laden with meaning even when we are prone to experience it as empty (Augustine, *City of God*, 11.26). *Responsive love* is attentive to that which is, and most attentive to that One who most fully is (Augustine, *Confessions*, 12).

Christianity celebrates human life as it actually exists in the presence of God, not merely as a human project of memory and imagination. Christianity views the present as the undivided and consummate nowness of God's own reigning and self-giving. Boredom therefore is viewed as a parasite on being, fed only by idolatry. The forgiveness and trust of which Christianity speaks make idolatry quite unnecessary and open the way for full reception and responsiveness to the present (John Chrysostom, *Homilies on Hebrews*, 22).

The forgiven and trusting person freed by the good news of God's coming is being invited to respond to the value-laden reality in which he actually stands. Human accountability at its deepest level is full responsiveness to the responsibility which God has taken for us on the cross, precisely amid our persistent irresponsibilities (Ambrose, *On Repentance*, 2.9).

In this way, Christian proclamation offers an end to idolatrous guilt in forgiveness, an end to idolatrous anxiety in trust, and an end to idolatrous boredom in responsive love. Christian freedom is freedom from idol-making sin, which spawns inordinate guilt, anxiety, and boredom (Luther, *Freedom of a Christian;* Calvin, *Institutes*, 3.2).

How does one ever come to learn to love the neighbor precisely within the confines of this present moment? How can the self

learn to overcome its egocentricity and become presently responsive to another's actual hurts and needs? To answer Christianly,
one must again tell a story, a history of events through which
God's own responsiveness to suffering humanity is made known,
enabling freedom for the neighbor (Ignatius, *Ephesians*, 14.1).
God's radical responsiveness to our suffering enables and invites
radical responsiveness to the suffering neighbor. That God *is*
love is the pith of the history of the crucified and risen Lord
(Gregory Nazianzen, *Orations*, 45).

Love is not the goal toward which Christian consciousness
strives, but that actual relationship which God invites us to receive and respond to now. Love is that actual relation to the
other to which the self is called, to be enjoyed and received each
moment of time (John Chrysostom, *Homilies on Matthew*, 42). I am
being called to serve my neighbor in his suffering need as God
has served me. There is an intrinsic connection between God's
care for me and my care for my neighbor (Gregory Nazianzen,
Orations, 43, 63). Christians hope that in ways beyond their seeing this concrete caring for the neighbor will have a healing
effect on the social process and ultimately on the course of history, to reclaim some small part of it, anticipative of its full re-
demption in God's own time *(Letter to Diogetus, 5,6)*.

Christianity's conception of social change has less to do with
political policy-making than with small daily acts of serving the
neighbor, the one-on-one relation with the suffering neighbor
(Augustine, *City of God*, 19). This does not mean that Christians
are uninterested in social policy. Christians have just as much
right in a political order to express their interests as anyone else.
But not more. In American society, there are Jews, Muslims, and
many sorts of Christians that differ politically. Baptists and
Catholics have a right to express themselves politically through

constitutionally provided channels, but they do not have a greater right than non-Christians, or those bored by religion.

A Personal Conclusion

I ended my Moscow lectures with a highly personal reference. Suppose I am drawn into adoring my daughter as if she were always going to be a final source of value for me, hoping vainly that she might be immune from finitude and death. Then suppose she is diagnosed as having a life-threatening cancer, a melanoma, which she was. Then this wonderful person, my daughter, having taken on the value for me of a center of value or a god, in being vulnerable to death, makes my whole life vulnerable to intensified anxiety. This is what I mean by the idolatrous intensification of anxiety. It is this anxiety that is overcome by trust in the giver of my daughter, and of all creaturely goods.

My daughter, who had been much on my thoughts that day, and in whom, as I said, I delight so as to be tempted to adore idolatrously, had asked me to bring her personal greetings to Soviet students. In the summer of 1987, in the days before the arms reduction agreements, Laura had walked from Leningrad to Moscow in an effort to reach out to Soviet citizens on behalf of peace. Deeply committed to person-to-person diplomacy and building the foundations of peace through interpersonal meeting, she had organized that great 500-mile Soviet peacewalk. I had promised her that I would greet the Soviets on her behalf, and wish them the blessings of peace. I am deeply proud of her for her willingness to take upon herself a lengthy journey, walking step by step into the heartland of provincial Russia. She met many people in rural villages who had never once seen an American. It was a moment of glasnost—anticipatory of the kind of openness that I keenly felt in the presence of Soviet students, and for which I am truly grateful.

The department chairman ended the session thanking me for my discussion of guilt, anxiety and boredom, and for an unpretentious clarification of the structure of awareness in time. The students, he said, were even more grateful that I told them about my daughter, Laura, whose picture all had seen, and who had already won their hearts by her courageous action. They were proud of her too. The next time I came to the Soviet Union, they told me in no uncertain terms, I was to bring her along with me.

Reaching
Out

The Spirit's Guidance amid Soviet Enigmas

Many, I knew, were praying every day for me during my time in Moscow. I felt prayers being answered unobtrusively and inexplicably. This is not an experience I often have, so I do not mention it routinely or flippantly. Just before I left Rome I was told that I would be in the daily prayers of the Jesuit faculty of the Gregorian University, praying in Italian. I also knew that evangelical colleagues in the United States were daily praying for me.

I was learning once again that even the most dismal and pathetic human situations can be fruitful, challenging and spiritually fertile. I was grateful to God as I trudged through the heavy snow. I worshiped constantly in Moscow. I awoke one morning to the radio strains of "Amazing Grace." Could this be Moscow? I wondered.

The further I proceeded the more I felt constantly preceded by grace amid the web of Soviet enigmas. Every step felt quietly shaped by providence. I was aware of the Spirit's guidance. How else could all this have happened? I wondered. It is difficult even now for me to think of the Soviet encounter without the premise of providence.

Nascent Friendships

Those days in the university were among the most consequential of my recent life. I made friendships I expect to continue. I hope that nothing I say here will cause them any grief. They reassured me that they expected me to tell the truth.

The professor who was my principal host had arranged a time for me to join him and his wife for a trip to Red Square. He is a tall, intelligent, quiet-spoken, cerebral academic; she a beautiful and thoughtful Armenian who grew up in Moscow. When I met her, I said instantly: "They said you were a beautiful woman, and they were correct." With their two-year-old child, they are forced by the housing shortage to live with in-laws. I was amazed to find that she, too, has a doctorate in religious studies. Her dissertation was on the social thought of the Russian Orthodox church in recent times.

I was wearing a crushable rain hat, which in Moscow weather looks very skimpy and unserviceable. I explained to my hosts that my wife had pled with me to throw the hat away before I left, but I had kept it because it fit perfectly in my coat pocket. My host said: "Your wife was right." I meant it looked ugly; he meant it didn't look warm enough. Concerned about my frosty ears in Moscow, the next day he brought me a generous present from his wife, a warm woolen hat to pull over my frosty ears. Such kindnesses were unobtrusively and frequently offered in Soviet life.

Soviet humor puts one in touch with both the despair and hope of Russia. At the entrance to the university there was a uniformed military officer in a small guardhouse. My host had his ID card in hand. When I asked whether I might need identification, he assured me that he would run interference for me. So I marched straight through the guardhouse without a word. My friend, in a jesting mood, apparently not wanting to show his card, and feeling annoyed by the whole humiliating exercise, pocketed his pass as he went through and said in Russian to the guard, "We are all Americans." We all tromped through the guardhouse without any slack in our pace. It probably would not have been funny a few years ago.

Later, when I noticed a young woman near the university smiling, I was just saying to myself, "Aren't the faces of Moscow wonderful?" when she burst out in a flat Nebraska accent: "Where ya' from?" Turns out she's studying philosophy and Russian in the "higher party school," which I learned was not the place where they have the best parties, but where they have for years trained foreigners on how supposedly to make the Communist Party apparatus work. Trouble is, only two types of foreign students remain at the school these days, she says: Laotians and Americans. Why? No one else seems to be interested in learning how to make the Communist system work. The Laotians come because they have no other educational options, and the Americans come because they are funded gratis by attractive exchange programs.

The varied competencies in this faculty brought frequent surprises. To give one example among many, I had lunch with another educator. He is a brilliant adjunct professor who had written his first doctoral thesis on Francisco de Suarez, the sixteenth century Spanish Jesuit theologian whose labyrinthine dogmatic and moral theology remains largely untranslated from the Latin. I learned that he had published a second book on types of theism, including classical theism, German theism, and process theism. He has another book now in the works on the future of metaphysics. Here was a Soviet religion scholar who was conversing freely with me in German and English, works easily in Latin scholastic sources, and who was raising many of the same sorts of questions that I would want to raise. He quoted freely from Alvin Plantinga, Hans Urs von Balthasar, Ian Barbour, Paul van Buren, Charles Hartshorne, Jerry Gill, Wayne Proudfoot, John Macquarrie and Ludwig Wittgenstein.

A poignant look came on his face when he mentioned that, since he was not a Party member, he had been forced some years ago to develop a special, adjunct relation as a visiting professor within this department of study. The implication was that at that time Party membership was presumed for those holding key teaching roles in the department of atheism. So he was not appointed there, but undertook a role in a scientific research institute where he has limited teaching responsibilities. However, he enjoys excellent library resources, where he works as a translator, researcher, and writer, in addition to occasional teaching. When I asked if he would ever travel abroad, he answered quickly that it was entirely out of reach. Nursing no regrets, he seemed completely reconciled to working in his research institute, happy that he has the coveted access to Western intellectual sources.

As I visited with him in the crowded university luncheon

room, I realized that our other faculty colleague had vanished looking for cigarettes. After living in a smoke-free environment, I once again realized how it feels to be back involuntarily in a smoke-filled room. Many there smoke, though cigarettes remain hard to come by. The antismoking sentiment has not yet stiffened.

Communication Snags
In trying to finalize arrangements for my arrival, I had written numerous unanswered letters. I had repeatedly attempted unsuccessfully to get through to a university FAX number scribbled in my datebook. Anyone who tries to go to the Soviet Union on a business visa should expect these kinds of impediments.

Only later when I arrived on the scene did I realize how intensely jammed are the Soviet communication systems. Mail is largely unreliable and often months late being delivered, if it gets delivered at all. I discovered that the huge humanities faculty offices were served by a single FAX machine that sometimes works, but more often is on the blink. The reason they did not telephone me back was that they cannot get lines out. The reason they did not write me was that my letters were not delivered. American have come to take these systems for granted as always up and running: telephones, express mail, electronic networks.

At times, I felt like I had landed on another planet. In the airport there was no paging system operating, so the person who had come to meet me missed me. He was later relieved to hear that I was safe in my hotel. He had been alarmed that I might have been waiting in a strange airport, feeling alienated.

Soviet Women Speak
Five of the religion faculty members were women. The women

students were not hesitant to speak of the status and role of women in the Soviet system, a subject in which I had special interest. I heard them argue plainly that Soviet women have remained through all this social dislocation basically happy, spiritually healthy, and inwardly centered. Soviet women think of themselves as strong, sensible, secure, and experienced in meeting obstacles. They do not collude with the temptation to feel that they are being victimized, as they see their Western counterparts colluding. They felt that they were more at home with their female identity than they perceived American women to be. I did not feel as deep a sense of alienation and blockage between men and women as in American society. They warned against any premature imposition of Western feminist values on Soviet society. "Let us find our own way," they said.

Women in the Soviet system have a long tradition of working. Since wartime days many have had child care provided. Many are in medicine, some in management and leadership roles, and some in politically influential positions. Most struggle with cramped housing and small budgets, and have menial, repetitious jobs. Many are engaging, intelligent, spirited women, not at all demoralized by circumstances.

When I reported to them that approximately one half of our Protestant ordinal candidates are women, they were astonished. I further pointed out that, while ten years ago most of my women students were radical feminists, now most are either moderate, restrained feminists or overtly disagree with many of the announced aims of feminism, with special concerns about the long-term costs of abortion on demand, the loss of identity of the nuclear family, and the supposed irreversibility of sexual experimentation and homosexuality. I found that Soviet women have great difficulty connecting with the mentality and aspirations of

American feminists, especially as caricatured in movies and media sources. The Soviet women students I talked with would be experienced as reactionary by radical women ordinands of ten years ago, but would resonate seasonably with most women ordinands today.

Why Empathy Is Required

Many stereotypes had to be quickly revised: that Soviets are humorless; that they respond like automatons; that they have become accustomed to oppression; that Soviet women are brawny; that Soviets have been so depersonalized by totalitarianism that they are all more or less alike.

Especially the notion that atheism remains a vital wellspring of Soviet policy is based on a gross misunderstanding. There is as much general boredom with atheism as with communism, and each seems to have taken the other down in a fitful dual drowning—with each trying to find footing on the other's head.

It is important for American observers to be patiently empathic and try to understand what has been happening to vulnerable families and neighborhoods during the long period of official Soviet police state atheism. We must not assume that the whole period was meaningless or purely demonic, with no redeeming elements or rational plausibility.

On Computer Technologies within Humanities Studies

The "Religion and Freethinking" departmental library for student use was thin and by Western standards antiquated, housed in a single dreary room containing tattered books mostly from the period of official Soviet atheism, with some from the older Russian Orthodox tradition, and virtually nothing from the West. They implored me to send books that I thought might be pertinent to their inquiries. I am sending a sizable shipment of books from my personal library. Many students read English, and some read German and/or French.

I gradually became aware through conversation that there were as yet no personal computers in the vast humanities department of Moscow State University. So I thought it useful to commend computer literacy in the humanities studies. The world of data banks and computers and digital technology lies straight ahead for them.

I explained that as a scholar in the humanities I had vigorously resisted computer technologies until 1980, because I thought digital computers were fundamentally alien to the analogical life of the mind, and to the kind of moral and aesthetic reasoning appropriate for humanities studies. I wrongly thought that a computer would only get in my way, cause me learning time and down time, and tend to make wooden any textual analysis to which I applied it.

Having now worked with computers for eleven years, I realize that there is much to be gained in humanities studies from the vast textual and research data bases that are readily available to us through computer technology, and becoming ever more available. They save me much more time than they cost me. Now I can work either in my office with my personal computer or at home with a modem attached to it. The modem connects my home and office computer system to the entire university library card catalog. From Drew's 400,000 titles, I can quickly identify bibliographical resources needed for a given project. I can send letters abroad with my computer through an international scholarly electronic network, and have them instantly delivered electronically over thousands of miles. More important, I have access to huge data bases through a CD ROM reader which sits beside my computer. I can search all the texts of ancient Greek literature for a particular word in minutes, a task which would have taken years if done by hand. It is like having an exquisitely indexed library of information, many hundreds of books, at my fingertips and stored in a single convenient compact disk.

Even if these advantages are not yet immediately available to Soviet humanities students, I urged them to be open to these newly emerging data bases and technologies, and to use them intelligently as they become available. I said this not to make them feel envious or guilty, but to encourage them to move promptly when possible. Within the frame of postmodern Christian consciousness, it is not inconsistent for humanities and religious studies to employ modern technologies self-critically. I found Soviet students more eager to venture into this arena than their teachers.

On Soviet Civil Religion

I asked how traditional sacramental concepts and symbols such as baptism, confirmation, penance, eucharist and last rites had been secularly reappropriated by civil religion within the period of official Soviet atheism. This led into an intriguing discussion on the degree to which Soviet civil religion is a reappropriation of Orthodox sacramentalism. I witnessed a thoughtful, searching exchange on whether the Protestant critique of medieval sacramentalism was analogous in special ways to the official atheistic critique of czarist Orthodox sacramentalism. This reassured me that this was not a faculty that felt compelled to speak with one voice.

There is a heated debate going on as to what a secularized "baptism" or initiation rite into the values of the Soviet civil order might mean, how it might be similar to and different from Christian baptism. I found them most interested in the category of civil religion, although among modern contributors to this question they seemed to be reading only Robert Bellah, not tougher voices like Will Herberg, Reinhold Niebuhr and Jacques Ellul. Baptism was being reinterpreted by some as a state function of initiation into identity formation, a public commitment to sharing in the values of society. I noted the structural similarity of this idea to Zwingli's view of baptism as a public act of confession of faith rather than a grace objectively conveyed.

At the very least the baptism debate indicates that traditional Christian metaphors still have vitality in the supposedly secularized imagination. But it was also depressing to realize that the actual profundity of Christian baptism was poised to be plundered by a desperately deteriorating, hypersecularized society. It made me wonder whether Christians should rejoice that the symbols of baptism have remained undiminished in power after seven decades of atheism, like seeds sprouting through the snow, or whether Christians should fight to resist the political captivity of these doctrinal definitions.

Sexual Risks and Hazards

The faculty expressed intense concern that impressionable Soviet young people might be too ready to take on wholesale certain dubious Western habits and values, from punk rock and porn to homosexuality and dope. I wondered if Soviet university students were hell-bent to try all the mistakes that American university students had been making the last seven decades. My guess is that some are likely to try. But it is a mistake to regard such experimentation as fated or a necessary phase.

With some I ventured into discussing the hazardous arena of the rising incidence of drug addiction, sexually transmitted dis-

eases and especially the recent American controversy over religious blessing of homosexual unions. They wanted to know how
I dealt with these issues theologically. With the increased influence of European sexual mores, movies and media, homosexuality appears to be growing in Soviet cities. Finding no way to
conveniently avoid a straightforward answer, I took a deep
breath and said: Since the definition of marriage is a sacramental
event, it comes directly within the legitimate range of classical
Christian teaching. Since anal intercourse and oral intercourse
between persons of the same sex cannot lead to generativity or
natural birth, classical Christian teaching views it as an oxymoron that persons of same sex could be in God's presence "mar-
ried." However, they may indeed have enduring friendships and
may, like all of us sinners, receive the forgiving grace of baptism
and eucharist. Christian marriage is by definition an enduring
covenant between one male and one female, grounded in the
potential gift of sexual generativity, a covenant which is enhanced by pleasurable sexual bonding.

Meanwhile the *civil* rights of those with "alternative sexual
lifestyles" must be vigilantly protected without conceding the
moral viability of their claims to social legitimation. "Christian"
gay-bashing is no more excusable than "gay" homophobe-bash-
ing. The term homophobia itself is a misnomer, I argued, since
it correctly refers to "panic over that which is *the same*" (homo =
same, *phobos* = irrational fear), not anxiety about anal and oral
sexual practices.

Our deepest political problems are not the natural or objective
hazards that have plagued humanity for centuries—starvation,
survival through drought, quakes, or uncontrollable disease—
but rather inward hazards that could be directly changed by the
right exercise of our own freedom. Our most hazardous illnesses

are often rationally amenable to free, responsible self-determination (as in alcoholism, sexually transmitted disease and drug overdose).

It is a key irony of modernity that the Acquired Immune Deficiency Syndrome, itself an evidence of distorted narcissistic freedom, has received American media and bureaucratic blessing as that special disease to which society must now give priority attention, even to the neglect of other diseases such as diabetes, cancer, Alzheimer's and malaria that affect so many more but which do not incidentally require sexual accountability to change. Short of a technological fix, there seems little resolution in sight to the crisis and challenge of AIDS, unless one thinks seriously of simple monogamous covenant sexual accountability. This remains the least attractive option to compulsive sexperimenters.

After decades of chemical and sexual experimentation we are now being led back to enduring sexual covenant in the presence of God. The recovery of our society from the suffering of these compulsive hooks is only possible on the basis of monogamous covenant fidelity in marriage. The rediscovery of joyful parenting is a key feature of postmodern consciousness.

CHAPTER
NINE

Sojourn
and Re-entry

*O*nce a philosopher built a huge country estate, as Kierkegaard's
parable goes—a castle with many rooms, furnished
marvelously with all possible comforts. But then the
philosopher lived not in the castle but in a tiny, foul outhouse
back of the castle. So today idealistic knowledge elites have repeatedly spawned and designed beautiful blueprint conceptualities while actually living in veritable outhouses. Those who have
chosen to live conceptually in an absolute utopia—a "no place"—
must now scrounge for some place to bed down. Kierkegaard's
parable was aimed at Hegel, who had built a spectacular theoret-

ical system but could not find a way to live in it. It applies to all modern utopias, whether socialist, behaviorist, humanistic, scientistic or demagogic.

There Was Once This Evil Empire

Though Marxism is dead almost everywhere in the Northern Hemisphere (except in diehard American university and isolated church coteries), the battle with Marxist fantasies continues to rage in Third-World countries with state monopoly communications networks where the people have little chance to hear of the demise of state planning everywhere else. Leninists have been unable to build an evil empire not because they didn't try, but because they have not yet learned to create wealth or engender individual accountability or stimulate productivity or generate even a decent modicum of consumer goods.

Everywhere the superregulated economy has been tried it has issued in demoralization, police states, an oppressive security apparatus, nonproductivity and poverty. So I have come to value the free market and a free society where open dialog is possible, based upon imaginative enterprise and the responsible free interplay of interests, constrained by democratically formed law.

Human self-assertiveness is always dangerous, but less so in the form of market exchange than that found in the form of rational planning by political elites, in which the planner's hidden interests is always the first thing planned. The democratic process, with all its tugging and pulling and assertion of special interests, is a more reliable expression of proximate justice than the fantasies of intelligentsia about how they would order all things rationally if given a chance. This is the Faustian game that knowledge elites forever dream of playing—suppose *we* had coercive power, regulatory power, planning power. The fantasy goes on, but has not ceased being dangerous.

As an erstwhile communitarian-pacifist-idealist it took me two decades to grasp just how evil were Marxist deceptions and dreams and police states. These have not suddenly stopped being evil just because they are now being popularly repudiated.

Soviet citizens know better than American liberals how precisely descriptive is the term "evil empire." Those who want to take away the moral judgment from the description are less in touch with Soviet suffering than those who have learned to call a gulag a gulag.

Civil Strife

It was a foreboding, ominous, portentous time to visit the Soviet Union. All agreed that it was a time of rapid disintegration and uncertainty. It is poignant to behold the patience of the suffering Soviet people.

There was always plenty for the tourists to eat, despite dire warnings that we might find ourselves in a food supply crisis. I had taken three cans of sardines and two Granola survival bars, just in case. But we had lots of chicken and beef and borscht and hard-boiled eggs, salami, cheese, hard wheat bread, marmalade and tea, and often ice cream. Meanwhile, I saw long lines of citizens waiting for food. On several occasions I was approached by beggars on the streets. Despite the widely felt experience of social malaise, however, I never felt life and limb endangered, as I do often on the streets of New York City.

Some thought civil war a possibility. I saw few signs that anyone would actually undertake such folly. Each time I heard the words "civil war" I felt a visceral response of anarchic dread. Some think it is coming and said frankly that it was a dangerous time to be in Moscow. I asked to which side the military would tilt in such a conflict. The answer was always toward keeping the empire together, and maintaining their own privileged position within it.

The faculty I talked with were as weary of both Gorbachev's *perestroika* and Yeltsin's new regionalism as they were of the ubiquitous military presence. They were relatively apolitical in so far as it might involve participatory action, but deeply concerned conceptually with current political developments. They feared that disintegrative forces would further erode social cohesion and incremental progress.

Soviet citizens want to be free but remain deeply ambivalent in their freedom. They are not yet sure how they wish to take responsibility for their future. Though searching for a new social order, they remain acutely dissatisfied with their own present order.

I was there during the momentous time when Yeltsin was challenging the central government, acidly calling upon Gorbachev to resign, with clumps of shouting demonstrators in Red Square. Seeing those demonstrators caused a picture to race across my mind, a picture of my daughter Laura, who with other Americans had unlawfully marched across Red Square with Soviet and American flags in a perfectly innocent but illegal demonstration in 1987, in one of the first unauthorized public protests in modern Red Square.

The View from the Tour Bus

I still find it ironic that the first places the foreign traveler is taken are those where the old religious order is much on display, with its beauty and serenity, its monks, its singing, its incense, its eschatological worldview, its colorful onion spires, its sense of transcendent presence, its ikons—all in such radical contrast to the stark functionality of modern Stalinist architecture which elsewhere dominates the visual horizon.

I found it paradoxical to realize that here I was in the epicenter of what used to be a Marxist society, acclimated and indoctrinated for seven decades to atheistic values, and yet the first place they wanted to take me and show me with pride was the holiest place of ancient Russian Orthodoxy, Zagorsk. It was as if we were stepping directly into the very past that they had sought for decades to repudiate and shame. At Zagorsk, I experienced the mysterious power and otherworldly beauty of an Orthodox mass. The sanctuary vibrated with booming bearded bass singers in unison. Prayers were offered with a fervency and intensity that jolted me. Everyone was standing (there were no seats) and the sanctuary was extremely crowded.

After the lectures, I had taken flight with a German-speaking tour group for a sightseer's view of the Soviet Union. Ironically, the Soviet Intourist system immediately channels Western tourists to their holy sites, where the guides interpret religion along the lines they had been taught years ago. Religion was suddenly once again being viewed as an unscientific superstition, in a language frame that seemed dated in comparison to what was obviously happening in the university.

At Zagorsk, as we listened to those solemn, beautiful deep voices chanting mass, we were urged by the Intourist guide to light a candle for good luck. I thought—how sad that "good luck" is all to be understood about this holy moment of eucharist. I was struck by the woodenness of the guides, their bondage to fading Soviet myths, their trivializing of religion, and their ponderous, practiced phrases.

The main road of Zagorsk, I mused, is the very street my daughter walked down to a cheering crowd in the Leningrad-to-

Moscow peacewalk of 1987. I felt a surge of pride as I realized that my spunky little daughter, who had insisted on studying Russian in college without any other sensible professional objectives, had gotten to Zagorsk five years before I did. What is more, she had walked there all the way from Leningrad. And she did this even with chronic edema in her leg resulting from cancer surgery. The ordinary people standing in the mass were surely some of the people who had greeted her so warmly along the street, I fantasized.

Church buildings which have for decades been used as museums—or for Communist Party functions, civil religion exercises or atheistic academies—are now gradually being returned to the purpose for which they were built. But I was depressed to see precious nineteenth-century icons for sale on the street. Some icons for sale were newly manufactured, but others were worn and frayed, having been apparently plundered from church or family treasures.

As I gazed at the Soviet world passing by through a frozen bus window, I realized that each time I cleared the window, I would get a few brief moments of clarity, then within seconds the fog would come and the window would glaze over again. This is how Soviet society seems to me—always glazing over just when you think you have a momentarily clear glimpse of it.

It was wonderfully uncomplicated just to sit back and ride in a bus and watch people out there in their struggle. I found it hard to be empathic with those in the cold. The tourist is kept at a proper distance from social reality. It is in a sense nice to be protected. The world passes by very painlessly for the touring subject, while the object of the tour, the object observed, the people in their pain and struggle, are not grasped or understood, and hardly in any way touched.

As I peered through the frozen window, I quietly mused that
it is winter in Moscow in more ways than one—winter for the
social process; deep winter for a struggling, uncertain society.
But spring is silently trying to push through the ice. Many spoke
of a society in deep trouble; some of possible civil strife; but none
of the old rhetoric of the Revolution.

The bus stopped. An announcement came that anyone who
wished could take pictures. The intent was to allow tourists to
step outside the bus and take pictures of a gleaming, distant
church spire. Only two got out into the deep freeze—a German
psychotherapist from Cologne and a German physician from
Hanover. When they trained their cameras on the distant spire,
they realized that unwelcome telephone wires were in the way.
They plunged impulsively across a ravine, not knowing how deep
the snow. Suddenly they were hip deep, then waist deep in snow.
This is Moscow in the winter of its discontent. It looks beautiful
and manageable, but everywhere there are hazards and sinkholes
far deeper than first imagined.

The Visual Scale
Everywhere in Moscow I was stunned by the immensity of the
architectural and social scale. There is a monumental proportionality and feel to all buildings, art, and statuary. The decor and
scale are huge, heroic, romantic, intimidating and intentionally
assertive. The scale is quietly making a statement about the diminished role of the individual in Stalinist society.

The enormous room in which we were standing as we talked
in the subway would be matched in the US only at places like
Grand Central Station or the old Atlantic City convention hall.
Everything Soviet seems to come in huge proportions. The
Izmailovo Hotel complex in which I was staying had four thirty-

story towers nestling 10,000 guests. There seemed to me to be only gigantic buildings in the Soviet Union, whether for offices or housing. Nothing was small or tight as in Japan. I saw no stand-alone family houses except in rural villages. The Aeroflot airline cabin was huge, the crowds huge, the subways huge, transporting thousands per minute. The scale of the university, like that of the society, is colossal. I often saw skis being carried on the subway not for pleasure but practically for getting around cross-country. Nothing in the economy seems to be working well except the subway system, though everything still works in spurts and groans. It costs only five kopeks, less than a penny, to go anywhere in Moscow on this vast metro system, whose dozen car units are often jam-packed, with another unit coming within three minutes. Yet long lines appeared wherever food was available.

There are a growing number of automobiles on Soviet roads, but proportionally far more trucks and buses than individual cars. I was surprised, however, to see an Audi advertisement on Moscow television that was blatantly addressed to an upwardly mobile capitalist audience, with an attractive woman driving a Mercedes that was skidding in the snow, then seen in an Audi dealership cheerfully exchanging her Mercedes keys.

The Rubles Trap

The Soviet market is chronically imbalanced with an abundance of deflating rubles chasing too few consumer goods. So there are lines everywhere, yet frustration that there is so little to buy at the end of the line.

It is hard to elicit private initiative when people have become accustomed to the steel borschtbowl. There is little motive for offering services or increasing production. With few incentives, there are few products, and fewer opportunities for exchanges. I did feel that recycling economies had gone a bit far when I realized that the toilet paper in the departmental restroom was hand-fashioned out of old graded exams, neatly cut into quarters.

The irony of tourist exchange in the Soviet Union is that one spends most of the time trying to figure out how to make minor exchanges for cheap, even junky, consumer goods. Once one has finally figured out how the exchange system works, there seems little time or energy left to make actual exchanges. Then one must spend as fast as possible to get rid of worthless rubles that are valueless outside of the Soviet command economy. The only ones who take the ruble seriously are those who live under its coercive rules. It epitomizes an unjustly planned economy always biased toward the interests of the planners. The not so hidden message: when you come to our planned economy, we care little about what anyone else thinks the currency is worth. We assign its worth here, and the bureaucrats will tell you how much we pay for dollars, regardless of market value. Everyone is expected to cooperate in this curious pretense. It might be dangerous to give offense.

The rubles trap is as amusing as it is frustrating for the foreigner. It is designed as a system by which foreign bearers of hard currency must buy and use inflated rubles, yet one finds it often very difficult to spend the rubles required by law. When I asked in the Rome airport before coming to Moscow to change dollars into rubles, the banker offered this grave rule: One year in jail for each ruble imported.

There are some places that take only rubles, and other places that take only hard currency. I had read in the Intourist brochure that rubles should not be taken in or out of USSR, but could be conveniently cashed in any Soviet airport. But when I tried to

cash rubles into dollars, even at the airport on the last day, no
one wanted them. So I just decided to spend them on merchandise. Still no one wanted them. I could not even purchase a Russian Pepsi. They wanted only dollars or German marks. The
Soviets are clearly sending the signal that they do not value their
own currency, and are blatantly determined to transform as
many tourist dollars into falsely inflated rubles as possible.

Nonetheless a primitive form of capitalism remains alive and
well among young, aggressive males constantly on the outlook
for any deal in hard currency. The popular Soviet mentality,
however, seems intractably ill-prepared to lay hold of a market
economy. Soviets are prepared for someone else to take care of
them. That is what they have been promised from the outset. It
may take fifty years or more to change these attitudinal patterns.
The struggle for a free market and political freedom seemed to
me to be quietly playing out in black market dealings on every
side street and alleyway.

Choice jobs in the tourist industry are those of hotel restau-
rant waiters, who have a rare opportunity to deal with the hard
currency of travelers. Otherwise, an effort is made to keep travelers completely away from all entrepreneurs except those approved by the state. So the tourists are herded around until
directed to specially approved hard currency shops.

To get money changed is like a game of mirrors. Every hotel
employee is instructed to repeat the official line: six rubles to one
dollar; yet everyone knows that the market exchange rate is
more like thirty rubles per dollar. Others in our group had ex-
changed dollars for rubles at a favorable rate. No one had approached me, and I did not ask, hoping to curb my aboriginal
tendency toward antinomianism. I was trying hard to follow the
rules and stay out of trouble.

The Trip Back

On the return trip from the Soviet Union, I stopped in Frankfurt, spent another week in Rome, and then returned to New York. Every seat in the huge Aeroflot Airbus was taken. No seats were assigned or reservable. So we chose seats in relation to our good or bad fortune in getting in line. High above the Soviet Union, I could not help but reflect on what was happening beneath the unsettled clouds, what storms were brewing for the population below. We flew from Leningrad over the Baltics, above the villages, streams, trees, far above the tiny objects below. The ungraceful Aeroflot, speeding through the sky, offered a fleeting panorama of the volatile historical situation I had just left.

The sun drew a thin bright line across the land on lakes, rivers, anything that reflected, as the plane labored toward Frankfurt. It is a meandering line composed of a thousand cataracts, springs, and lakes clutched in the hills. The hills shed the gleaming water, the valleys receive it, the descending sun illumines it from above. It could be Iowa just as well as Poland.

I held Rome and Moscow in my prayers. Both cities have a long memory of hierarchical rule. Both are mother cities, pilgrimage cities. I wondered if I was making a postmodern Protestant pilgrimage from the prototypical city of modernity to the prototypical city of premodernity. Rome worships. Moscow wonders curiously what worship is and why it has such strange power. Moscow is confused and disoriented by its own immobilized freedom. Moscow is deteriorating socially. Rome is thriving, though amid much inefficiency. Only in the Frankfurt airport stopover did I remember how it was to be in a place where everything once again seems to work. The bathrooms, the telephones, the food service.

While Rome has the patina of the eternal city, Moscow the

stark look of the archetypal modern city, Frankfurt exhibits the
paradigm of the secularized Protestant city. I was puzzled to find
a chapel in Frankfurt Airport right next to what was called the
"Sex Shop," about whose function I dared not inquire.

The unexpected snow appeared suddenly on the far side of the
rim of the Alps. Inside the rim it was white; outside a dark green.

Only on the trip back from the Soviet Union did I glimpse a
startling headline that revealed what had been going on the previous day in the world below. An all-out ground attack had been
launched by coalition forces in Kuwait. It was a moment long
expected. I prayed that it would not be a lengthy combat. I prayed
for both friend and foe, and for the intelligent use of reason and
conscience even in times of absurdity and peril.

As I flew over the Italian Riviera, the Alps retreating, the sun
setting, I prayed for the peace of the troubled world, a speedy end
to conflict and more just resolution of the recalcitrant conten-
tions that brought about the present military struggle. I asked
God for guidance myself, that I might use the same good judgment that I wished others to exercise.

The day insists on receding. A darkening reddish-purple band
separates the retiring day from the emerging night, from the
darkening water, from the blackening sky. The waters are a deep
gray blue, the skies a blue-graying white.

Earth, light, water, air—all elements join to retint the dimming
sky with darkening earth. Everything stands under the inexorable command of the ebbing evening. This day seems ready for the
night. This day does not resist the darkness or pretend to assert
the absurd wish that light should continue. It yields, even as my
alertness yields. Without earth there is no cup to hold the waters
that cover the earth; without water, no refreshment for the
struggle of plant life; without plants no animal sustenance; with-

out these no human life.

So praise be to Thee, Thou giver of air, earth, fire, and water, without whom are no creatures, no finite values whatever. Forgive our sins and save us from our follies.

Epilog:
Renaming the
Second World

*T*he Leningrad to which I returned six months later had already been renamed St. Petersburg, not after the seventeenth-century genius of imperial power but the first-century saint. The renaming of St. Petersburg (which occurred the day before our arrival there) was a hotly debated issue. Its result was already being interpreted as a shift of consciousness toward the Christian tradition now being recovered after the most brutal repression of modern times. It represented a vindication of those seeking to re-identify the long-suffering Christian heritage of the lost years.

The Soviet Union to which I returned had largely dissolved into constituent Republics. As I entered the Soviet Disunion, no one knew exactly what country we were in, or even its proper name. There was no longer a Soviet Union to speak of in the cohesive formal sense. The center did not hold. Jerry-rigged arrangements were being Scotch-taped together to keep the semblance of union, while the real vitality was breaking up into the separate republics and city councils. The secessionist sentiment was like a flood.

The Moscow to which I returned was already in the post-Soviet era, having disavowed Marxist theory and Leninist prac-tice in seemingly irreversible ways. Intimidating statues of KGB chief Dzerzhinsky, Stalin and Lenin lay horizontal in the park. It was a graveyard of fallen idols, one of the most poign-ant sights I saw there. I walked around their supine forms without anxiety, as if a bad dream were over. It was only then clear to me that the old coercive society was truly gone and a new democratic process was emerging, overflowing with the cacophonous sounds of freedom.

I was able to observe the expiring Soviet moment five months before its lingering demise, then three weeks after its death and resurrection. It took an arcane theory of providence to even try to explain the dialectical meanings of the abortive Koup Klutz Klan. An entire social order was not merely dete-riorating, but disappearing—disintegrating before my eyes.

A new consciousness was being born but had not yet taken more than a primitive fetal shape. The new birth does not yet give more than vague hints of how it might in time impact history. But it is entirely certain of what it is leaving behind, and does not want ever to recur. The uncertainties of early 1991 were transmuting into the certainty of change in the late summer, and the mixed despair and hope of the fall. Some were grieving over irrecoverable losses of prestige, power and secure identity, while others were rejoicing over the gift of a new future. I saw Moscow in a moment of intense transition, yet felt that it thereby was mirroring the human situation generally.

The Vulnerability of Civil Order

The civil and social situation I entered was very unstable and corrupted, at times dangerous. Only half the mail ever arrives. Low-paid police turn their backs when a crime is being committed. If they arrest the offender they could be shot, or if lucky bribed. When a robbery occurs, the arresting officers may get an offer that is hard to refuse. The law is selectively enforced, if at all. Crime and anomie are increasing.

Also bribable: housing officers, sanitation workers, bureaucratic gatekeepers of every sort in every corridor of governance, and yes, even health workers—we were told that patients often are forced to bribe nurses for food and medicine. To hear some tell it everyone is bribable.

This elicits dangerous scenarios even for pampered Americans whose hard currency is most lusted after. We were told that at certain times of the night in some places of the city anarchic possibilities were latent, though personally I never felt any loom directly.

The old Soviet system was based on coercion, with heavy state police power at every turn. The new consciousness lacks the heavy-handed Leviathan. The pendulum has swung toward every person's hand being turned potentially against every other person's hand. Like a body without an immune system, this is a social, moral and economic environment that has a hard

time fending off corruption, intolerance, protectionism, bully-
ing and graft.

It is a sad commentary on freedom that license accompanies
it. There is more thieving, prostitution, pornography and un-
disguised self-assertiveness in the new consciousness than in
the old. It makes it almost seem attractive to some to return
to the old, to be petrified of freedom, to yearn for the stability
of the defunct totalitarianism.

As one new Russian acquaintance put me in a 25-ruble cab,
which he thought was 22 rubles too much, he said sadly: "This
is the price of freedom. When you get freedom, you risk the
abuse of freedom. Without freedom you do not have its
abuses."

It is not going from bad to worse to go from the KGB to
occasional muggings, from an established police state mafia to
a privatizing mafia. But we can take some comfort that anarchic
experimentation never lasts forever. It inevitably tends toward
some re-establishment of social equilibrium.

The Economy in Rapid Transit

Even where there are stated prices, there is often rancorous
dickering, especially if hard currency is involved. Imagine you
were in an economy where few goods are available, where food
and merchandise appear sporadically and are stolen from
stores. Your task comes down to how to feed your family. It
is a daily hunt. The lines are long, and there is no deliberation
or choice at the end of the line, only a brief exchange.

Eventually this will settle into a more stable pricing and trading system, but now it is very hard to find anything one wants
at a price one can pay. Too few goods are being chased by too
many rubles which have little value. This encourages consumer

hoarding and distribution-system profiteering. This is not yet a free market in our sense, which requires contracts, banks, loans, credit, reliable timing for delivery of goods and services, reasonably stable and advertised prices, and no widespread bribery.

The economy is experiencing a negative growth rate. In 1989 it was a two-per cent negative growth rate, in 1990 five per cent; next year perhaps a fifteen- to twenty-per cent negative growth rate. Inflation could spring from double digit to a thousand per cent hyperinflation before long. This would be a devastating social experience, particularly for those with fixed incomes, as we saw in Germany after World War 1. Even amid the current anomie, many show extraordinary kindness, however tempted they are to yield to cynicism.

The Treasury of Suffering
The consciousness of our Russian hosts was intensely focused upon understanding their own historical and private suffering. Theologically, they were into theodicy.

Their suffering has become a profound treasury of hard-won experience that has quietly elicited spiritual growth and deepening reflectiveness. No one would wish another to suffer, but when it does regrettably occur, it is possible that it can bring one closer to God, who suffers with humanity in the incarnate crucified Son.

Hedonic narcissistic Americans do well to learn from that wellspring of arduous experience, and not presume to teach Russians an elementary course in Spirituality 101. Our own materialistic culture is far more deeply corrupted than theirs in many ways. There is little room for boasting. Those emerging out of seventy-three years of atheism may be more open to the address of God through the suffering neighbor than we in pious and secular America.

Even though people were killed in the atheistic oppression, we were told the image of God in them was not harmed. Many have learned what it means to suffer for righteousness' sake. That stamps the human spirit with a special beauty. It clarifies intentionality, deepens the spirit, challenges idolatry. The spiritual treasury of Soviet Jews and Christians and Muslims can now be offered to the rest of the world.

Cherished Faces and Voices

I found it important to listen empathically to the voices of Russia, even if they were a bit crazy, like my New Age friend's engrossed concern to save the natural quartz crystals. I wanted to listen intently to absorb the emotive depth of what he and others were expressing. We must not be afraid to listen to them, even in their distortions.

There were wonderful, beautifully sculpted eyes and brows and rippled faces among the elderly of the Russian village church we visited. The young had radiant, intelligent faces, but the old had carved, hammered faces, wrinkled with suffering and time. Their eyes reveal that in patience they have preserved their souls. Among some there is a steeliness and distance and non-disclosure in their deportment and body language, and a hopeless sense of alienation in their eyes, so sad to look into that they look away.

Among the special spiritual gifts of the era of darkness are the capacity for humor ("What else did we have in our absolute limitations?" said one), mutual support of friends in need, the special joy that comes simply from survival, and endless conversation often under clandestine conditions. The talk has no practical result, but that only leaves it all the freer to form and play. This once subterranean dialog is poised today for an open burgeoning of ideas. It is like a sudden spring where everything is simultaneously erupting. It is April in Moscow and the buds are pushing through dirty ice. Sunshine peeks through wee holes.

Soviet and American partners in dialog found that they needed first to listen empathically to each other for those insights and resonances and possibilities that would show us how our religious traditions might provide the courage required to reinvent aspects of our two changing societies. We listened intently to each other to discover how the religious imagination might once again intensify moral sensibilities and deepen historical awareness, and enlarge attentiveness to the needs of those long neglected. We sought to grasp how the religious life might conceivably supply the vast energies needed to renew a troubled nation. It is time to ask how the greatness of God, as known by Jews, Christians and Muslims, can bring humility, self-criticism and realism to our efforts.

Keeping the Faith

There is nothing that better describes the present Soviet situation than the religious categories of providential guidance through the hazards of history, prevenient grace being offered amid sin, sinners standing under final judgment, idolaters seeking the grace of repentance, penitents seeking atonement for sins, prayer for true conversion and faith in the grace of God—these arguably are the most consequential events going on now in the Soviet soul.

The former Soviet Union is arguably the most intentionally atheistic experiment ever launched in history. Yet God was

ceaselessly worshiped during the worst decades of brutal repression. No amount of viciousness or cruelty could stamp out
faith in God. Prayers were raised daily amid the drab silence of
a police state. Theologically this stands as powerful testimony
to general revelation, and to the teaching of the common grace
that seeks the salvation of all, and the prevenient grace that
precedes repentance, and the doctrine of *preparatio evangelica.*

The YHWH, WHO IS incomparably, according to Jewish and
Christian recollection, is now acting to bring national consciousness to the grace of repentance and a new awareness of
the hedgings of divine providence, so as to enable once again
the life of faith, hope and love. God the Spirit has accompanied
the harrassed families of the workers' paradise.

The intractable destiny of Russians the world over has been
to suffer, whether they were on side of communists or Jewish
or Christian believers or bystanders. This suffering has extended to the diaspora network of Russians, Ukrainians and
Armenians abroad. Extended families have suffered, whether
in Brighton Beach or Paris or Kiev, not only within the pale but
around the world. This attests the theological principle of vi-
carious suffering: that we do not suffer merely for our own
sins, but for others'. Theodicy becomes all the more knotty
when I suffer for your sins, and you for mine.

The Attempted Destruction of *Ekklēsia*
The churches were blown up to make way for subway systems.
At each subway stop I prayed for the children of those deprived
of churches blown up in order to build the subways. This is an
ugly paradigm of ironic modernity. They bought a more effi-
cient transport system, but at a terrible price. Now the Moscow
metro serves as the capillaries and veins and lifeblood of the

city. Meanwhile Christians cannot forget that it stops at places often where churches were blown to bits and considered entirely dispensable. Only now is the society relearning how indispensable were the churches to the moral cohesion and future of a durable social process.

We were taken to the site of one of the greatest churches in prerevolutionary Moscow, now in a quiet park near a metro stop. After the revolution they tried to dynamite the church and it refused to yield. Again and again they blasted it unsuccessfully, so much that it became known as the church that would not succumb. Finally the dynamite succeeded, and when the communists tried to build a giant stadium to celebrate Lenin's revolution, the foundation began sinking. Again they relaid the foundation, and built the huge stadium, and it again began collapsing of its own weight. Christians took this as a sign that if the church was destroyed, the regime would not be successful in building anything else there for idolatrous purposes. After several unsuccessful attempts at reconstruction, the site is now a benign Olympic swimming pool.

Baroque churches were used for grain storage, industrial units, bureaucratic offices, atheistic museums, Pioneer youth groups. The guiding principle was utility mixed with state vainglory, a principle which Soviet architecture embodies to a fault. Only in retrospect can we see that, in time, every effort to demean the religious tradition has come to nothing.

Dependency and Infantalization

Poignantly the bright, youthful, bearded leader of a lay theological academy in Moscow described post-Soviet society as disabled, its citizens victimized by their environment. This touched a special chord in me, and I challenged him, perhaps unfairly, using the psychologist Viktor Frankl as a model. Frankl had discovered the strength of his character and personal identity precisely in a Nazi concentration camp. Was he a victim, or had he refused to be inordinately victimized?

August 19 meant the will to resist, the courage to say no to all previous victimization. Those who refused to be victimized were the intrepid young people who faced the tanks at the Russian Parliament, the "White House." They were not willing to be infantalized, to collude with their victimizers.

I was not denying the fact of victimization, but pointing to the degree to which one cooperates with it as one's own personal choice. Only in choosing not to be victimized do I discover my soul more deeply and patiently. We as adults cannot be treated as children unless we agree to be treated as children.

Some were willing, others unwilling, to be invalids. Some elected to cooperate with deceivers, others not to collaborate, even at great cost. The Christian tradition of martyrdom and the period of early Christian apologetics of the first three centuries attests the spiritual power of the refusal of idolatry. Those who have colluded with their victimization are slowly awakening to the fact that they must now take initiative on behalf of their own interests.

The Spiritual Rebirth of Russian Christianity

The seventy-three years of darkness are regarded by Jews and Christians with historical perspective as a relatively short time compared to eternity, or even to the four millennia of Jewish survival or ten centuries of Russian Christianity.

When our translator, Irene, as a girl of fourteen went to the school library and asked to read the Bible, she was hushed up, and was told it would not be good for her future career as a teacher to read it. During the oppression, people were afraid to go to church because the KGB wrote down the names of all who received baptism or holy communion, then harassed them at work. Many in the early phase of perestroika did not believe that they could safely go to church. They watched and waited during the years of 1985 to 1989. In last three years, and especially since the putsch, they regained confidence that they would not be harassed if they attended church. It is this change of consciousness that has changed their behavior. There is a stunning absence of surveillance.

People are freely giving money to restore churches which had been stripped to the walls. They are seeking to support educational programs, rebuild hospitals, orphanages and charitable institutions outlawed for seven decades. Now when a church building is received back by the churches from the government, they seek to repair it, open it up, and immediately it is overcrowded. In 1980 there were ten churches in St. Petersburg, attended mostly by elderly women; now there are sixty—crowded with young people. Anyone who says only old people are going to church is five years behind the present situation.

People are attending church not in huge but significant numbers. The ecclesia is no longer merely a tiny pariah remnant of society. The church is among the few institutions not only surviving the present disorder but being strengthened in it.

Freedom without God, as Dostoevski knew, has been found to be hazardous to human health. Freedom to do anything without conscience or constraint is perilous. Post-Soviets now feel their freedom muscularly, but with an equal awareness of the potential hazards of freedom abused. Without religion, it has been found to be more difficult to achieve justice, mercy and humility than the Enlightenment optimists imagined.

We were asked not to forget who it was that killed thousands who believed in God: hyperidealists who imagined they were promoting equality and the rationality of economic redistribution. Through it all, faith was passed quietly down from mother to daughter, grandfather to grandson. The church was being chastened and deepened, but never denied the possibility of grace. It is now being resurrected. Even in its darkest days, belief in God continued quietly. Christians knew that the iconostasis (a wall or screen covered with icons) in some churches remained standing, even if draped or scarred. They could not worship publicly, but as long as the iconostasis was there in the padlocked church, they did not lose heart.

Though the streets were full of the blood of those who believed, God did not ever die in our memories, they said. Though the Bible was banished, we kept it silently in our hearts. Without belief in God we could not have persevered. Governments come and go, but the people stay. You cannot kill everyone. A new birth of faith is occurring after decades of darkness.

Church Restoration and the Opportunity to Believe

Relief in the form of food supplies should be made available, provided it is offered through relatively non-corruptible channels. Which is more urgent, we asked, church restoration or teaching ministries or food and clothing relief? To our surprise we learned from our partners in dialog that they thought that food was not more important than teaching and learning, or eating more than receiving the bread of life. They need nothing more urgently than the opportunity to relearn to believe. Post-Soviet Christians told us it is incorrect to assume that they need material food more than spiritual food. That is a part of the materialistic determinism they are now disavowing, and trying to get off their backs.

They know that their grandfathers believed in God, and that their fathers did not believe in God. Now they are clear that they do not believe in Communism, but whether they are to believe in God as a generation is yet to be decided. It is a decisive, open question. Many are, for the first time in their lives, eager to inquire. It is a moment of exceptional opportunity for the teaching of religion.

So when their young people go to the museums to see the great works of art of Byzantine Russian Christian history, they see portrayals of Adam and Eve, Cain, Abraham, Moses, Jeremiah, the nativity, the evangelists, the saints and so forth. But they do not understand much of what the imagery means, having had no opportunity to learn the rudiments of the Christian tradition. This is why basic religious education is such a high priority. They need church-school teachers and religious educators as much as anything else. It is as important to bring education into the church for young people, as it is to bring the church into ancillary public-school education, which some cities now have on a voluntary basis. They cannot do this without supplies, teachers, books, printing operations, curricula and buildings. They are now trying to get their buildings and charitable institutions back in decent repair and working order, but the obstacles are overwhelming.

The restoration of the churches is going to require the sweat and financial sacrifice of ordinary people with very limited fiscal resources. That small gifts are increasing is seen as evidence of their great reservoir of belief, and compared to the widow's mite. With capital assets so hard to come by, these people would not support the church voluntarily if not urgently committed to it.

It was argued that technological gifts will have the biggest bang-per-kopek consequences for teaching ministries. They need computers, copiers, fax machines, reliable telephones, recorders, overhead projectors, VCRs, films, paper clips, and above all books and printing materials that will help them engage in their mission of education. The profound tradition of Russian philosophical spirituality is now resurrecting after decades of eclipse. Books banned for decades, like those of Berdyaev, Bulgakov, and Soloviev, now must be republished. Access to publishing and to foreign libraries has been highly controlled and limited.

In America we have plenty of empty church buildings and need to fill them with people. In Russia they have the people, but not the buildings. Church growth is burgeoning, while we are trying to devise desperate strategies for church growth. There many are ready and wishing to go to church, but the churches are not yet opened, books and Bibles not available, the materials and paper and communication networks not there. The churches of these two worlds need to find ways of becoming more catholic, more universal, attentive to each other ecumenically.

When American Protestant liberals visit the Soviet Union, they sometimes echo the line that it would be unecumenical if they were involved in preaching or teaching ministries, and that our efforts must be limited to charitable or compassionate ministries for the homeless and sick. This is a false dichotomy for Russian Christians, who do not see theological teaching as separable from charity or sacrament.

We pigeonhole these more easily than they. We need to get over the fixed habit of invariably offering the cup of cold water *without* the name of Christ, without any testimony to God's mercy. That does not connect with the present needs of Russian Christians for moral and spiritual education.

One Moscow political science professor argued that maybe the church will soon wind up again in disrepute if people pin all their economic hopes on it, and it fails to produce material comforts. Will the church then be on the defensive again, assuming that what people most want is economic betterment?

The answer came rapidly in sharp tones from other Russian participants: No—spiritual renewal is seldom correlated with economic riches, but rather it is sorely tempted by wealth. Even without economic prosperity, they said, the churches are poised to grow exponentially, provided they offer the required moral leadership to society. Faith, they said, is not dependent upon the fickle contingencies of the material future. Even if economic crisis persists, it will not dim the vitality of the emergent confessing church.

It is ironic that with all the official atheistic energy spent *against belief*, the atheists were only willing to grant the right to life on the basis of a *belief* in their system. They coercively required absolute faith in the strained Marxist-Leninist rhetoric to which so many American academics and ecclesiastics remain sentimentally attached. Meanwhile the totalitarians denied any other faith legitimacy, even to the point of refusing the right to life to any who believed otherwise, in an enormously corrupted pretense of absolute equalitarianism.

The Babylonian Captivity of the Colluding Church

Soviet Christians do not hesitate to distinguish between the true church and the collusive church. They seem to know the exact difference between suffering saints and safe hierarchs. The witnessing, confessing church bears few similarities with the idolatrous church. Sharply distinguished in their minds was the actual church of faith from the pretended church of civil religion, which has proved willing to take favors from genocidal atheists under the curious pretense that it had to be done for the good of religion.

It is rightly called the Babylonian captivity of the colluding church, as distinguished from the costly Babylonian freedom—the freedom to confess—of the living body of Christ. The end of that captivity occurred on August 19 to 21, 1991, after seventy-plus years of oppression, like the seventy-plus years of captivity of Israel in Babylon (586-515 B.C.). As Shadrach, Meshach and Abednego refused to give consent to the Babylonian idolaters, many Russian saints freely withheld their obeisance to idolatrous, atheistic ideology. A deadly history of martyrdom resulted which is yet to be recounted accurately. A twentieth-century hagiography is needed for the saints of Russian martyrdom under communism.

The Call to National Repentance

Since we were not there, we cannot rightly see or judge the moral dilemmas of the hierarchs. But the Russian Christians who did suffer have a right to say that the legitimacy of the apostolic tradition has been tarnished by the hierarchs' complicity, and that their KGB collaboration calls for repentance.

Had we been in their shoes, we might well have fallen into the same temptations. So let us not be too harsh on hierarchs who had tragic choices. They achieved one goal, apostolic continuity. Unless I can answer that I could have done better had I been in their shoes, I have little ground morally for judging them unambiguously.

But I must convey the moral power of the claims of confessing Christians who spoke quietly and poignantly of the true repentance of the whole country and of all who colluded, including us. They are asking for a new spiritual beginning, cleansed of desperate and tragic perfidy. They know already the decisive importance of repentance to faith. This issue brings Christians back to the basics of confession of true baptismal faith, renunciation of the demonic, and the turning decisively away from idolatry.

Repeatedly, without prompting, we heard from Russian voices the sober call for national repentance. They have been punished for their sins, they told us again and again. It is a biblical reading of their current history. Their national ordeal was a punishment for sin, of colluding with social evil, of not finding the means of throwing off the yoke of demonic oppressors, and not keeping their religious life free. They do not need Westerners to teach them some deep sense of guilt, for they are already deeply aware of it. It is their conscience that addresses them, not ours, which rightly is addressed to us.

An Ecumenical Lesson
The World Council of Churches has sadly played into the Soviet civil religion collusion with a long history of defending not the saints or laity or dissidents but the establishment in bed with party apparatchiks and KGB, a pattern that has persisted even into the maturing years of perestroika.

From confessing Christians we learned that the WCC we had been trusting had played its role in unwittingly legitimating the old oppressive order. The bravest and most thoughtful persons we met there were intensely disillusioned with world ecumenism as represented by the WCC. Even in their critique of the hierarchs' collusions, our friends had remained faithful to the

Russian Orthodox faith, but knew its leadership had been conned by KGB manipulators. They also knew that human rights issues had been systematically ignored by the liberal churches of the West, whitewashed both by Soviet and ecumenical bureaucrats on behalf of a Faustian ecumenical bargain.

This taught me a decisive ecumenical lesson: When we as ecumenists ignore human rights realities or set them aside on behalf of a cheaper and easier collusion with established powers, we deface the apostolic tradition and disavow the holiness and catholicity of the church.

The Ethics of Survival

A trenchant debate continues among serious religious minds and Spirit-formed people on the ethics of survival and the gospel of suffering. The issue: To what degree is it justifiable to cooperate with idolatrous authorities when no options but sacrifice seem open?

Some argued it as morally necessary for the church to cooperate with totalitarian oppressors in order to maintain its bare continuity and identity. How could the church even survive without some collusion? Some think the church's cooptation by the authorities was justifiable proportional to the circumstances, about which Americans should not be quick to judge. Even the hierarchs who colluded were still doing the best they could under difficult circumstances in which few options were open. Meanwhile it is claimed that the hierarchs helped perestroika because the political leaders had imagined the church to be waning in the West, while the WCC helped to show that the church was still alive and to be dealt with. That is the position of the apologists for the colluding church.

Others from the confessing church point to the plain fact that the KGB found ways of manipulating the church for decades. As former KGB chief Oleg Kalugin said candidly: "We controlled the church for almost seventy-four years. The lay people would be surprised at how many of their priests were our agents, reporting directly back to us, or when they reported to the holy synod it was faithfully transmitted to us." The WCC collusion with the Soviets was now being openly viewed by the confessing church as analogous to the Catholic concordat with Hitler. Pimen was viewed under the analogy of the Jewish collaborators who handed over the names of Jews to Nazi persecutors.

The alternative was to refuse to collaborate at the cost of enormous suffering. Those who refused perfidy paid a tragic and terrible but to them morally obligatory price. The actual suffering of nameless confessing laity was deep and unforgotten. It has built enormous strength of character into the body of Christ, the *laos* of Russian orthodoxy, but at great cost. Untold numbers have died or wasted away in Siberia. These voices and those who represent them express their aversion and loathing of the ecclesial colluders.

Whatever the merits of these arguments are to those who had few options, no one can deny that the WCC had many options. So for the ecumenical bureaucrats to enter into this cooptation when other options were open was thought strategically regrettable by some, and morally unforgivable by others. American inheritors of a "liberty or death" tradition of political vigilance chose neither liberty nor death but cooptation.

The Faustian Bargain

In return for the WCC toning down its resistance to Soviet religious repressions, the ecumenists had the satisfaction of the continued inclusion of the huge Russian Orthodox church in the WCC. The KGB was willing to play along with Patriarch Pimen if he and his synod would help them with Soviet foreign policy objectives. Pimen and the WCC played the game strictly according to Marxist KGB rules, not mentioning the unmentionable, that religious repressions continued even through the waning days of perestroika. The religious liberty laws remained on the books but were not enforced. So the hardliners could always say: Just look at our wonderful laws that provide complete religious liberty. The WCC played along with that deception by blessing Pimen and welcoming his blessing.

The new Patriarch, Alexi II, was at one time also snug with the KGB and considered safe. Since the failed coup he has apparently shown more independence, but his ingenuousness is doubted.

This is why democratizing laity and priests ask modestly, in Christian candor, for a sincere spirit of repentance among hierarchs for years of party collusion. Many Orthodox parish priests now have serious doubts that it is conscionable for the Russian Orthodox Church to remain associated with an ecumenical body that in their minds symbolizes collaboration.

The Silence of the Protestant Mainline
The Protestant oldline churches, including my own United Methodist tradition, have been laggard in understanding the Soviet situation. We have focused on ecumenical posturing at a time when we might have offered substantive ministries of compassion and witness, including the proclamation of the gospel through broadcast ministries. We repeatedly chose not to engage in these ministries because they were perceived as evangelical tasks below our dignity, as preaching ministries not

well fitted for our social gospel tradition. Thus we wind up with a poor record in ecumenical political cooptation.

Some in the confessing church argue for Russian Orthodox withdrawal from the ecumenical movement unless by some strange providence the ecumenical bureaucrats might come to true repentance, which they show little likelihood of now understanding. I see little evidence from WCC and NCC middle-level bureaucrats that they are in the mood of radical repentance that we found among post-Soviet Christians.

Where were the Presbyterians, Episcopalians, and United Methodists in the struggle for religious liberty in the Soviet Union during the period from the Khruschevian persecution to the present? Inadvertently in complicity with the KGB, by deferring to the hierarchs and the WCC political manipulators who preferred that Protestants not rock the boat by being involved in preaching or teaching or available broadcast ministries of any sort on the Soviet airwaves. Broadcast ministries have continued in short wave throughout the repression, but none to my knowledge has been openly supported by liberals, who have a bad conscience to begin with about Christian testimony.

That supposed ecumenical courtesy has blocked us from preaching and teaching ministries desperately needed by a society that was brutally prevented from teaching Christian truth. We are wholly deprived of the excuse that proclamation was impossible, for the Uniates and evangelicals and Pentecostals continued to preach and meet throughout the oppression, however high the cost.

Meanwhile the gospel was needed but had no practical means of delivery because of our indebtedness to ecumenical politics and bureaucratic incest. It is a denial of real ecumenism that we were systematically and *by our decision absent* from the Soviet Union in its time of greatest need.

This is an embarrassment for Methodists, for whom preaching and charitable and educational ministries have always been linked, not bifurcated. Mission-sending agencies must now do penance by breaking through this ecumenical barrier to support broadcasting and publishing ministries, churches, teaching ministries and schools. Protestants can now share without inhibition in the building of schools, hospitals and orphanages, but ecumenical habits die hard. There is as yet little movement in that direction. We continue to defer even at this late date to the Patriarchate and the WCC bureaucrats. If we have no voice it is by our own repeated choice. The Protestant laity have not protested. Not many seem to be aware of these pathetic facts. It is a wonder someone has not blown the lid.

The collusion has remained intact even after the coup because we find avoidance easier than confrontation. Criticism has not been allowed among politically correct bureaucrats who wish to stay cozily in the inner ecumenical circle. The critics are driven as far from 475 Riverside as possible. Those drawn into the vacuum are even at this late date poised to rehearse once again the sentimental rhetoric of Marxist idealism.

What the Islamic tradition has best to give the Soviet society is its own deep Islamic faith. Similarly, what mainline Protestants had to give would have been their Protestant faith. But it has been disastrously withheld from the Russian ethos.

Admittedly this is a moral issue about which reasonable persons differ, but I feel called to deliver the message I heard from the confessing church without dilution of the passionate tone in which it was addressed to me.

Large graffiti letters scrawled on the base of a seated statue of Marx summed it up: *Workers of the world, forgive me.*

Selected Bibliography

Further Reading on Religion in the Soviet Union

Alexeyeva, Ludmilla. *Soviet Dissent.* Middletown, Conn.: Wesleyan University Press, 1987.

Berdyaev, Nicholas. *The Origin of Russian Communism.* Ann Arbor, Mich.: University of Michigan Press, 1960.

Billington, James H. *The Icon and the Axe: An Interpretive History of Russian Culture.* New York: Random House, Vintage Books, 1970.

Bociurkiw, Bohdan R. *Ukrainian Churches under Soviet Rule: Two Case Studies.* Cambridge, Mass.: Harvard University Ukrainian Studies Fund, 1984.

Bourdeaux, Lorna, and Michael Bourdeaux. *Ten Growing Soviet Churches.* Bromley, Kent: MARC Europe, 1987.

Bourdeaux, Michael. *Risen Indeed: Lessons in Faith from the USSR.* Crestwood, N.Y.: St. Vladimir's Seminary Press, 1983.

Buss, Gerald. *The Bear's Hug: Christian Belief and the Soviet State, 1917-86.* Grand Rapids: Eerdmans, 1987.

Conquest, Robert. *The Harvest of Sorrow: Soviet Collectivization and the Terror-Famine.* Oxford: Oxford University Press, 1986.

Curtiss, John Shelton. *The Russian Church and the Soviet State.* Boston: Little, Brown, 1953.

Elliott, Mark, ed. *East European Missions Directory.* Wheaton, Ill.: Institute for the Study of Christianity and Marxism, 1989.

Ellis, Jane. *The Russian Orthodox Church: A Contemporary History.* Bloomington, Ind.: Indiana University Press, 1986.

Fletcher, William C. *Soviet Believers: The Religious Sector of the Population.* Lawrence, Kans.: Regents Press of Kansas, 1981.

Gorbachev, Mikhail. *Perestroika: New Thinking for Our Country and the World.* New York: Harper & Row, 1988.

Handbook for Christian Travelers to the USSR. Wheaton, Ill.: Slavic Gospel Association.

Hebly, Hans. *Eastbound Ecumenism*. Lanham, Md.: University Press of America, 1986.

Hill, Kent R. *The Puzzle of the Soviet Church: An Inside Look at Christianity and Glasnost*. Portland, Ore.: Multnomah, 1989.

Jarvesoo, Elmar, and Tonu Parming, ed. *A Case Study of a Soviet Republic: The Estonian SSR*. Boulder, Colo.: Westview Press, 1978.

Neformalniye: A Guide to Independent Organizations and Contacts in the Soviet Union. Seattle, Wash.: World Without War Council, 1990.

Nesdoly, Samuel. *Among the Soviet Evangelicals*. Carlisle, Penn.: The Banner of Truth Trust, 1986.

Pospielovsky, Dmitry. *The Russian Church under the Soviet Regime: 1917-82*. 2 vols. Crestwood, N.Y.: St. Vladimir's Seminary Press, 1984.

Religious Prisoners in the USSR. Keston College: Greenfire Books, 1987.

Sawatsky, Walter. *Soviet Evangelicals since World War II*. Scottdale, Penn.: Herald Press, 1981.

Simon, Gerhard. *Church, State, and Opposition in the USSR*. London: C. Hurst, 1974.

Solzhenitsyn, Aleksandr I. *The Gulag Archipelago, 1918-1956*. New York: Harper & Row, 1985.

————. *Letter to the Soviet Leaders*. New York: Harper & Row, 1975.

Spinka, Matthew. *The Church in Soviet Russia*. Westport, Conn.: Greenwood Press, 1980.

Szczesniak, Boleslaw, ed. *The Russian Revolution and Religion: A Collection of Documents Concerning the Suppression of Religion by the Communists, 1917-25*. Notre Dame, Ind.: University of Notre Dame Press, 1959.

Voobus, Arthur. *The Martyrs of Estonia: The Suffering, Ordeal and Annihilation of the Churches under the Russian Occupation*. Stockholm: Estonian Evangelical Lutheran Church, 1984.

Walters, Philip. *World Christianity: Eastern Europe*. Monrovia, Calif.: Missions Advanced Research Communication Center, 1988.

Weigel, George. *Must Walls Confuse?* Washington, D.C.: Institute on Religion and Democracy, 1981.

Will, James. *Must Walls Divide? The Creative Witness of the Churches in Europe*. New York: Friendship Press, 1981.

Journals: *Door of Hope; The Explorer; Freedom at Issue; Frontier; Keston News Service; New World Outlook; Prisoner Bulletin; Religion in Communist Lands; The Right to Believe; Ukrainian Quarterly; World Parish*.

Further Primary Readings in Classic Christian Writers

All ancient Christian references may be found either in the Ante-Nicene Fathers, edited by A. Roberts and J. Donaldson (10 volumes), or in A Select Library of the Nicene and Post-Nicene Fathers of the Christian Church, edited by H. Wace and P. Schaff (28 volumes, New York: Christian, 1885-1900, reprinted Grand Rapids, Mich.: Eerdmans, 1979), referenced by book and chapter or section number. I have given patristic references in their tightest form, simply by section and subsection. Biblical references unless otherwise noted are from the New International Version.

Among major collections and continuing series of translations of patristic writers since 1950 are

Ancient Christian Writers: The Works of the Fathers in Translation. Edited by J. Quasten, J. C. Plumpe, and W. Burghardt. 44 vols. New York: Paulist Press, 1946-.

Classics of Western Spirituality. Edited by Richard J. Payne et al. 30 vols. to date. Mahwah, N.J.: Paulist Press, 1978-.

Corpus Christianorum. Turnhout-Paris: Edition Brepols, 1953-.

Creeds, Councils and Controversies. Edited by J. Stevenson. London: SPCK, 1966.

Creeds of the Churches. Edited by John Leith. Richmond, Va.: John Knox Press, 1979.

Documents in Early Christian Thought. Edited by Maurice Wiles and Mark Santer. London: Cambridge University Press, 1976.

The Early Christian Fathers. Edited by Henry Bettenson. New York: Oxford, 1956, 1972.

Early Christian Writers: The Apostolic Fathers. Translated by Maxwell Staniforth. London: Penguin Books, 1968.

Enchiridion Patristicum. Edited by M. J. Rouët de Journal. Rome: Herder, 1951.

The Fathers of the Church: A New Translation. Edited by R. J. Deferrari. 69 vols. to date. Washington, D.C.: Catholic University Press, 1947-.

Later Christian Fathers. Edited by Henry Bettenson. New York: Oxford, 1956, 1972.

The Library of Christian Classics. Edited by J. Baillie, J. T. McNiell, and H. P. Van Dusen. 26 vols. Philadelphia: Westminster, 1953-1961.

A New Eusebius. Edited by J. Stevenson. London: SPCK, 1957.

Sources crétiennes. Edited by Henri de Lubac and J. Daniélou. Paris: Ed. Du Cerf, 1941-.

The Syriac Fathers on Prayer and the Spiritual Life. Introduced and translated by Sebastian Brock. Kalamazoo, Mich.: Cistercian Publications, 1987.

Further Readings in Postmodern Orthodoxy

When I speak of the renaissance of patristic studies generally, and of postmodern orthodox writers since 1950, among those I have in mind are the following:

Altaner, Berthold. *Patrology.* New York: Herder and Herder, 1961, from the 1938 German ed., Freiburg: Herder.

Archer, Gleason L., Jr. *Jerome's Commentary on Daniel.* Grand Rapids: Baker, 1958.

Balthasar, Hans Urs von. *The Glory of the Lord.* 7 vols. San Francisco: Ignatius Press, 1982.

Bouyer, Louis. *A History of Christian Spirituality.* 3 vols. New York: Harper & Row, 1982.

Breck, John. *The Power of the Word.* Crestwood, N.Y.: St. Vladimir's Seminary Press, 1986.

Campenhausen, Hans von. *Fathers of the Greek Church.* New York: 1959.

Chadwick, Henry. *The Early Church.* New York: Penguin, 1967.

Cross, F. L. *The Early Christian Fathers.* London: G. Duckworth, 1960.

Danielou, Jean, and Henri Marrou. *The First Six Hundred Years.* New York: McGraw-Hill, 1964.

Dulles, Avery. *The Survival of Dogma.* New York: Doubleday, 1971.

Dvornik, Francis. *The Ecumenical Councils.* New York: Hawthorn, 1961.

Ellul, Jacques. *Living Faith.* San Francisco: Harper & Row, 1983.

Florovsky, Georges. *Collected Works.* Cambridge, Mass.: Nordland, 1972-.

Frend, W. H. C. *The Rise of Christianity.* Philadelphia: Fortress, 1984.

Goodspeed, Edgar J., and Robert M.Grant *A History of Early Christian Literature.* Chicago: University of Chicago Press, 1942, 1966.

Grant, Robert M. *Augustus to Constantine.* New York: Harper & Row, 1970.

Greer, Rowan A. *Broken Lights and Mended Lives: Theology and Common Life in the Early Church.* University Park, Penn. Pennsylvania State University Press, 1986.

Grillmeier, Alois. *Christ in the Christian Tradition.* London: Mowbray, 1965.

Hopko, Thomas. *Worship.* New York: Department of Religious Education Orthodox Church in America, 1976.

Howard, Thomas. *Evangelical Is Not Enough.* Nashville: Thomas Nelson, 1984.

Jedin, Hubert. *Ecumenical Councils of the Catholic Church.* New York: Herder and Herder, 1964.

Jenson, Robert W. *The Triune Identity: God According to the Gospel.* Philadelphia: Fortress, 1982.

Kannengiesser, Charles, ed. *Early Christian Spirituality.* Philadelphia: Fortress, 1986.

Kelly, J. N. D. *Early Christian Doctrine.* London: A & C. Black, 1958.

Lindbeck, George. *The Nature of Doctrine: Religion and Theology in a Postliberal Age.* Philadelphia: Westminster, 1984.

Lonergan, Bernard. *The Way to Nicaea: The Dialectical Development of Trinitarian Theology.* London: Darton, Longman and Todd, 1976.

Lossky, Vladimir. *The Mystical Theology of the Eastern Church.* London: J. Clarke, 1957.

Meyendorff, John. *Christ in Eastern Christian Thought.* Crestwood, N.Y.: St. Vladimir's Seminary Press, 1975.

Muggeridge, Malcolm. *Confessions of a Twentieth-Century Pilgrim.* San Francisco: Harper & Row, 1988.

Neuhaus, Richard John. *The Catholic Moment.* San Francisco: Harper & Row, 1987.

Norris, Frederick W. *Faith Gives Fullness to Reasoning: The Five Theological Orations of Gregory Nazianzen, A Commentary.* Leiden: E. J. Brill, 1991.

Norris, R. A. *Manhood and Christ: A Study in the Christology of Theodore of Mopsuestia.* London: Clarendon Press, 1963.

O'Collins, Gerald. *The Second Journey.* New York: Paulist, 1978.

Outler, Albert C. *The Christian Tradition and the Unity We Seek.* New York: Oxford University Press, 1957.

Pelikan, Jaroslav. *The Emergence of the Catholic Tradition* Vol. 1 of *The Christian Tradition:*

A History of the Development of Doctrine. Chicago: University of Chicago Press, 1972.

Pelikan, Jaroslav. *The Spirit of Eastern Christian Thought.* Crestwood, N.Y.: St. Vladimir's Seminary Press, 1975.

Quasten, Johannes. *Patrology.* 4 vol. Westminster, Md.: Christian Classics Inc., 1983-84.

Ratzinger, Joseph. *The Feast of Faith.* San Francisco: Ignatius Press, 1981.

Sellers, Robert V. *The Council of Chalcedon.* London: SPCK, 1953.

_____ . *Two Ancient Christologies: Alexandrian and Antiochian.* London: SPCK, 1953.

Voll, Dieter. *Catholic Evangelicalism.* London: Faith Press, 1963.

Wallace-Hadrill, D. S. *Christian Antioch: A Study of Early Christian Thought in the East.* Cambridge: Cambridge University Press, 1982.

Webber, Robert E. *Common Roots.* Grand Rapids: Zondervan, 1978.

_____ . *The Majestic Tapestry: How the Power of Early Christian Tradition Can Enrich Contemporary Faith.* Nashville: Thomas Nelson, 1986.

Webber, Robert, and Donald Bloesch, eds. *The Orthodox Evangelicals.* Nashville: Thomas Nelson, 1978.

Wilken, Robert L. *The Myth of Christian Beginnings.* Notre Dame, Ind.: University of Notre Dame Press, 1980.

DATE DUE / DATE DE RETOUR

SEP 0 1 1994			
SEP 1 3 1994			
NOV 1 5 1994			
OCT 1 5 1996			
FEB 1 5 1997			
MAR 0 3 1997			
MAR 1 1 1997			
OCT 2 1 1997			
MAR 0 5 2001			

CARR M^cLEAN   38-297